THE PALESTINIAN AUTHORITY, ISRAEL AND THE PEACE PROCESS: WHAT'S NEXT?

HEARING

BEFORE THE

SUBCOMMITTEE ON
THE MIDDLE EAST AND NORTH AFRICA

OF THE

COMMITTEE ON FOREIGN AFFAIRS
HOUSE OF REPRESENTATIVES

ONE HUNDRED THIRTEENTH CONGRESS

SECOND SESSION

MAY 8, 2014

Serial No. 113–146

Printed for the use of the Committee on Foreign Affairs

Available via the World Wide Web: http://www.foreignaffairs.house.gov/ or
http://www.gpo.gov/fdsys/

U.S. GOVERNMENT PRINTING OFFICE

87–838PDF   WASHINGTON : 2014

For sale by the Superintendent of Documents, U.S. Government Printing Office
Internet: bookstore.gpo.gov   Phone: toll free (866) 512–1800; DC area (202) 512–1800
Fax: (202) 512–2104   Mail: Stop IDCC, Washington, DC 20402–0001

COMMITTEE ON FOREIGN AFFAIRS

EDWARD R. ROYCE, California, *Chairman*

CHRISTOPHER H. SMITH, New Jersey
ILEANA ROS-LEHTINEN, Florida
DANA ROHRABACHER, California
STEVE CHABOT, Ohio
JOE WILSON, South Carolina
MICHAEL T. McCAUL, Texas
TED POE, Texas
MATT SALMON, Arizona
TOM MARINO, Pennsylvania
JEFF DUNCAN, South Carolina
ADAM KINZINGER, Illinois
MO BROOKS, Alabama
TOM COTTON, Arkansas
PAUL COOK, California
GEORGE HOLDING, North Carolina
RANDY K. WEBER SR., Texas
SCOTT PERRY, Pennsylvania
STEVE STOCKMAN, Texas
RON DeSANTIS, Florida
DOUG COLLINS, Georgia
MARK MEADOWS, North Carolina
TED S. YOHO, Florida
LUKE MESSER, Indiana

ELIOT L. ENGEL, New York
ENI F.H. FALEOMAVAEGA, American
  Samoa
BRAD SHERMAN, California
GREGORY W. MEEKS, New York
ALBIO SIRES, New Jersey
GERALD E. CONNOLLY, Virginia
THEODORE E. DEUTCH, Florida
BRIAN HIGGINS, New York
KAREN BASS, California
WILLIAM KEATING, Massachusetts
DAVID CICILLINE, Rhode Island
ALAN GRAYSON, Florida
JUAN VARGAS, California
BRADLEY S. SCHNEIDER, Illinois
JOSEPH P. KENNEDY III, Massachusetts
AMI BERA, California
ALAN S. LOWENTHAL, California
GRACE MENG, New York
LOIS FRANKEL, Florida
TULSI GABBARD, Hawaii
JOAQUIN CASTRO, Texas

AMY PORTER, *Chief of Staff*   THOMAS SHEEHY, *Staff Director*
JASON STEINBAUM, *Democratic Staff Director*

———

SUBCOMMITTEE ON THE MIDDLE EAST AND NORTH AFRICA

ILEANA ROS-LEHTINEN, Florida, *Chairman*

STEVE CHABOT, Ohio
JOE WILSON, South Carolina
ADAM KINZINGER, Illinois
TOM COTTON, Arkansas
RANDY K. WEBER SR., Texas
RON DeSANTIS, Florida
DOUG COLLINS, Georgia
MARK MEADOWS, North Carolina
TED S. YOHO, Florida
LUKE MESSER, Indiana

THEODORE E. DEUTCH, Florida
GERALD E. CONNOLLY, Virginia
BRIAN HIGGINS, New York
DAVID CICILLINE, Rhode Island
ALAN GRAYSON, Florida
JUAN VARGAS, California
BRADLEY S. SCHNEIDER, Illinois
JOSEPH P. KENNEDY III, Massachusetts
GRACE MENG, New York
LOIS FRANKEL, Florida

CONTENTS

THE PALESTINIAN AUTHORITY, ISRAEL AND THE PEACE PROCESS: WHAT'S NEXT?

THURSDAY, MAY 8, 2014

House of Representatives,
Subcommittee on the Middle East and North Africa,
Committee on Foreign Affairs,
Washington, DC.

The subcommittee met, pursuant to notice, at 1:47 p.m., in room 2172, Rayburn House Office Building, Hon. Ileana Ros-Lehtinen (chairman of the subcommittee) presiding.

Ms. Ros-Lehtinen. The subcommittee will come to order.

After recognizing myself and Ranking Member Deutch for 5 minutes each for our opening statements, I will then recognize other members seeking recognition for 1 minute. We will then hear from our witnesses.

And, without objection, the witnesses' prepared statements will be made a part of the record and members may have 5 days to insert statements and questions for the record, subject to the length limitation in the rules.

The Chair now recognizes herself for 5 minutes.

Last July, Secretary Kerry, together with negotiators from Israel and the Palestinian Liberation Organization, PLO, announced that the Israeli-Palestinian peace negotiations had restarted.

Here we are now, 9 months later, and what do we have? We have a peace process that fell apart, yielding no positive results, leaving both parties with an even greater distrust of one another.

In fact, the legacy of this failed round of talks could be that it ended up causing more harm than good, as it seemed to have moved Fatah and Hamas closer to reconciliation while Abu Mazen continues his push for de facto recognition at the U.N., both of which will have serious repercussions for U.S. policy toward the Palestinians.

There are laws on the books that prohibit U.S. assistance to any U.N. Agency that accepts a nonexisting state of Palestine amongst its ranks. And though the administration continues to seek a waiver in order to give the funding, I will continue to do everything in my power to ensure that it does not get this authority.

And then there is the Palestinian Anti-Terror Act, a bill that I authored that eventually became law that prohibits U.S. assistance to a Palestinian Government that would have Hamas—any members of Hamas amongst its ranks.

Should reconciliation happen and Hamas become a part of the Palestinian Government, I fully expect Secretary Kerry and the administration to enforce the letter of the law.

I don't doubt Secretary Kerry's earnestness in wanting a mutually beneficial deal between the parties. I share that earnestness. I don't think anyone in this subcommittee would disagree.

But from the beginning, I questioned the prioritization of this endeavor in light of so many other pressing matters in the Middle East and the North African region. To say that this task was one better suited for Sisyphus would be an understatement, forever pulling that rock up the hill.

Secretary Kerry's faith that Abu Mazen and the PLO could sit down with Israel this time and somehow come to the table with a new-found desire to actually achieve peace with Israel was misplaced.

The P.A. and Abu Mazen have shown time and time again that it is a corrupt entity, incapable of governing the territories, unwilling to see a two-state solution in which two Nations could exist side by side in peace.

And so one has to question the amount of time, effort, and resources spent chasing the unobtainable, at least under the present conditions, when there is one of the worst humanitarian disasters in recent history occurring in Syria, transition to democracy impediments in Egypt, and Iran continues its support for terrorism worldwide and its nuclear ambition have not waned.

Over 150,000 people in Syria have been killed while millions have fled to neighboring countries or have been internally displaced, and the administration's policies, undefined and indecisive, have failed to adequately address this issue.

According to the State Department's recently released global terrorism report, Al Qaeda and its affiliates are on the rise and becoming more aggressive in places like Iraq, Syria, Yemen, and North Africa.

Iran continues to be the world's foremost state sponsor of terrorism, actively targeting Israeli and U.S. interests, increasing its presence in our own hemisphere and Africa, and, of course, it is still propping up the Assad regime in Syria, all of this while the administration continues to negotiate with the regime in Tehran over its nuclear ambitions, even though State's own assessment is that Iran continues to refuse to prove its nuclear program is indeed for peaceful purposes.

And these are just a few of the fires that need to be put out in the Middle East and North Africa region. Yet, the failed peace talks have managed to fan the flames.

The signed reconciliation agreement between Fatah and Hamas signifies that Abu Mazen is more interested in making peace with terrorists than it is with Israel, but it reveals who Abu Mazen really is. He is a man who has never been a true partner for peace, but, rather, an obstacle toward peace.

Abu Mazen is a man more interested in taking U.S. taxpayer money and using it to pay salaries of convicted Palestinian terrorists with Israeli and American blood on their hands than he is in running an effective government that could lay the foundation for an independent state.

Abu Mazen is a man who is corrupt and uses cronyism to maintain his position as the head of the PLO and the P.A. and fears losing that control and, thus, will never make the hard decisions for the benefit of the Palestinian people at his expense.

This hearing is important to understand how and why this latest attempt at peace between Israelis and Palestinians failed and allows us to take a closer look at the real obstacles to peace in order to better formulate U.S. policies as it relates to the P.A.

And I am now very pleased to yield to my ranking member and good friend, Mr. Deutch of Florida.

Mr. DEUTCH. Thank you, Madam Chairman.

Thanks to our witnesses for being here today.

It is a special honor for me to welcome Congressman and former chairman of the Europe Subcommittee, Robert Wexler, back to this committee. I will have more to say about him in a couple of minutes.

Earlier this week marked Yom Ha'atzmaut, the 66th anniversary of the independence of the State of Israel. Since her independence in 1948, Israel has defended herself on every single one of her borders.

Despite facing continued, even existential, security threats, Israel has become a vibrant democracy, one that, unlike so many of Israel's neighbors, respects human rights and religious minorities, all while an innovative, high-tech economy flourishes.

We must acknowledge that the Palestinian Authority under President Abbas has made tremendous strides in working to build state institutions and establish security forces that have dramatically reduced violence in the West Bank. The United States Congress has committed a great deal of resources to strengthening the Palestinian Authority, to the tune of $400 million per year.

At the outset of peace talks last August, Secretary Kerry worked with the international community on a $4-billion economic package that would help jump-start the Palestinian economy, because we all know that a stable state starts with a strong, thriving economy that provides greater opportunity and prosperity for the Palestinian people.

For the past 9 months, the world watched as Secretary of State Kerry and his team worked feverishly to restart direct negotiations between Israel and the Palestinians.

Now the April 29th deadline has come and gone without any agreed-upon framework or extension of talks, which leads to the obvious question: What happens next? What role should the United States play going forward? And what are the consequences if Fatah reconciles with Hamas?

We hope to see progress in the talks. We hope to see two States or two peoples arising out of direct negotiations and without the imposition of any third-party plans.

But we cannot expect Israel to continue to negotiate with a partner who has chosen to reconcile with a terrorist organization that refuses even to recognize Israel's right to exist, one that targets innocent Israeli civilians with rockets and suicide attacks.

President Abbas claims that any interim government will abide by the same principles the PLO adheres to, which have been stipulated by the international community: Renouncement of violence, recognition of Israel's right to exist, and the acceptance of all previous diplomatic agreements.

Let's be clear. Israel will not negotiate with any Palestinian Government that is backed by Hamas terrorists and refuses to accept the Quartet Principles.

Any government that includes Hamas terrorists will not receive U.S. assistance. The law is clear. And this Congress will not allow U.S. Funding to flow to any government that includes terrorist members of Hamas.

I hope this message has been received in Ramallah because, like so many of my colleagues here, I believe in U.S. assistance to the Palestinians.

If we want to see a thriving, stable state for all Palestinians, economic support and foreign investment is the best way to promote peace and stability.

Why would President Abbas jeopardize the world's support by partnering with terrorists? It is easy to sit back and say we have seen this before. As we know, there have been similar failed reconciliation attempts in 2007, 2011, 2012.

But the damage the Palestinians do in trying to unify with a terrorist group is that the Palestinians aren't using their time to build their institutions and to prepare their people for peace and for the recognition of the State of Israel.

Aid dollars are needed for all of those things, whether it is for security, institution-building, education, or economic growth.

So the bigger question is: What is Abbas doing to really make a Palestinian state viable? What is he doing to make a Palestinian state that can be stable?

Instead of unifying with a terrorist organization, why not take a very positive and concrete step? Condemn violent acts of incitement.

He can also prevent incitement and prepare for peace by taking a small, but very significant, step: Put Israel on the map, his map. Official Palestinian Government maps must show Israel.

That will communicate to the Palestinian people that Israel is here to stay and that those who envision a Palestinian state, as they put it, from the river to the sea, whether they are members of Hamas or whether they are anti-Israel members of BDS groups, do not support a two-state solution, a Jewish and a Palestinian state. By changing the maps, President Abbas can show that he is committed to peace even while they are not.

Now, we know the only path to a peaceful two-state solution is through negotiations between both parties. Unilateral actions will never achieve this goal. I hope that there is still space for negotiations to continue without this unity deal.

And so, as Abbas stands at this very critical juncture, I urge him to choose the real partner in peace.

And I yield back.

Ms. ROS-LEHTINEN. Thank you very much for that opening statement.

I now would like to yield to our members for their opening statement.

And we will start with Mr. Chabot, subcommittee chairman. Thank you.

Mr. CHABOT. Thank you very much, Madam Chair.

Unfortunately, I have another hearing that I have to attend here shortly. So I will read the testimony of all the panel members here following the hearing.

But I did want to come over to personally recognize and acknowledge the presence of our former colleague, Congressman Wexler, who served this institution so honorably for so many years.

And we actually served not only on Foreign Affairs Committee together, but, also, Judiciary Committee, and we participated in such things as the impeachment of a President. We were on opposite sides on that one.

Mr. WEXLER. On everything.

Mr. CHABOT. Well, on everything. I stand corrected.

Although we were two of the co-founders of the Congressional Taiwan caucus. So we generally agreed on issues with respect to Taiwan.

And I remember a number of codels that we were involved in and did, I believe, good work in various parts of the world.

We went to The Hague together when Israel was under such attack around the world for trying to defend itself in building a security fence in some areas, walled in other areas. And they were getting much criticism, and we were there speaking out on their behalf.

I remember meeting with President Mubarak in his office when he was still in power in Egypt, and we were urging him to hold free and open and fair elections. And perhaps, had he followed our advice back there, he would find himself under different circumstances today.

But, in any event, I appreciated his service to this institution, and we appreciate his good work on behalf of this Nation at this point in his capacity.

And we welcome you back.

And thank you, Madam Chair. I yield back.

Ms. ROS-LEHTINEN. Thank you so much, Mr. Chabot.

Mr. Higgins of New York is recognized.

Mr. HIGGINS. Thank you, Madam Chair.

I just wanted to also welcome the panelists here. And just to take this in a little bit different direction, if you look at public polling, both the Palestinians and the Israelis in equal numbers, 70, 80 percent, believe in a two-state solution.

But, at the same time, by those same percentages, they don't think that a two-state solution is possible; so, what you have is a context of disbelief.

And, you know, unilateralism, one side taking a move, doesn't move us closer to any kind of solution. What you need is mutual steps here.

What could the Israelis do to demonstrate to the Palestinians that they believe that the West Bank, or most of it, should be part of their state? Well, don't build outside of the blocks.

You know, the blocks represent about 8 percent of the West Bank. You would be saying to the Palestinians, ''We are only going to build in the area that we think should be our state, not the area that should be your state.''

If a parallel move is made on the Palestinian side, what could the Palestinians do? As my colleague Ted Deutch had said, put Israel on a map.

You know, if you ask the Palestinian leaders why Israel isn't on a map, they say they don't know what the borders are. Well, you know what they want them to be.

So, you know, there is no Web site, there is no textbook, that talks about, you know, the existence of Israel in a two-state scenario.

The other is, as Ted also said, stop the incitement, you know, stop treating Palestinians that kill Israelis as martyrs. This creates a cycle of violence that transcends generations.

You know, in my tradition, in the peace process in Northern Ireland, you know, both sides that had committed themselves for 30 years to violence, on the Catholic side and the Protestant side—before they were admitted to the negotiating table, both sides had to renounce violence. Both sides had to participate in the destruction of their arms to demonstrate that they were truly committed to a peaceful coexistence.

And I think what we have to accept here is that you can do all kinds of negotiations. You can try to bring the leaders together to push them in a direction that they don't want to be. But a settlement to this long-standing issue has to come from within. It is not going to come from without.

And, you know, the two sides—you know, the United States can push Israel, push the Palestinians, together, but both have to come to the conclusion that, you know, their disdain for each other historically is not nearly as important as their love for their own children and the future of a two-state solution between the Palestinians and the Israelis.

With that, I will yield back.

Ms. ROS-LEHTINEN. Thank you very much.

And if the subcommittee would indulge me for just a minute, Mr. Rohrabacher, I am going to turn to Mr. Deutch, who is going to say—I would like for him to say a few words about Mr. Wexler. And I know you have some other commitments.

And I do as well, but I know that Mr. DeSantis is going to take over for me. We have got a meeting with the Syrian opposition group.

So Mr. Deutch is recognized, Mr. DeSantis and then——

Mr. DEUTCH. I am sorry that we both need to head off to other commitments. And, as our witnesses know, we will pay close attention to the testimony today both as you deliver it and written.

I just wanted to take a moment to welcome my friend and my former congressman, Robert Wexler, back to this committee on which he so ably served for so many years.

It is Congressman Wexler's commitment to these issues, his expertise about these issues, his deep passion not just for what happens in Washington, but for the constituents that he represented that I now have the good fortune to represent—it is all of these things that made him a tremendous Member of this body.

And the way that he forged relationships with members on both sides of the aisle, as we have already seen here today, is a high bar that he set that I have spent the past number of years trying to reach.

So it is wonderful to have you have here. You are doing great work, Robert, in your current capacity at the S. Daniel Abraham Center. I wanted to thank you for all that you have done while you were here, all the great work that you continue to do. It is an honor for us to have you here.

And I also wanted to acknowledge Danny Abraham, who is also here, who is a World War II veteran, a great American entrepreneur, and someone who has dedicated so much of his life to making peace as well.

Robert, it is a pleasure to welcome you back.

Danny, it is a pleasure to welcome you to the committee.

And, Mr. Chairman, I will yield back to you.

Mr. DeSANTIS [presiding]. Thank the gentleman.

The gentleman from California, Mr. Rohrabacher, recognized.

Mr. ROHRABACHER. Yes. I would like to associate myself with the remarks that were just given us about our former colleague and friend.

I have been following this, as many Americans have, the possibility of having peace in the Middle East for, well, almost my whole life now. I was born in 1947, and I guess Israel was born in 1948.

I do not believe that this is a problem where—at least it isn't anymore—where you have two sides that are unwilling to try to reach out to one another.

What we have is Israel in the last 20 years has given up territory, has reached out, has, in fact, given up the West Bank and has permitted a total of the Gaza Strip to go under the jurisdiction of the Palestinians.

And I see that, in the last 20 years, 30 years, we have seen Israel give up a lot and I haven't seen the Palestinians give up anything. What have they given up in the last 20 years?

The only thing that stands today between peace in the Middle East, as far as I can see—and I will be anxious to hear your reaction to this—the only real thing that stands between peace is a Palestinian willingness to say, ''We don't have the right to return to the pre-1967 borders. Thus, we do recognize Israel has a right to exist as a separate state and we will have the two-state solution.''

But every time I ask a Palestinian—and I have lots of Palestinian friends—''Well, that means that you agree that this right of return doesn't exist. Because if you say the right of return, you are saying Israel doesn't have a right to exist as an Israeli—as a Jewish state. Right?''

And so they never will say that. To me, that is the only thing that is a roadblock. The Israelis have already made concessions. What concessions have the Palestinians made? They are not even willing to make that.

I am for peace. I really am. I am not—I don't think of myself as someone in favor of Israel over the Palestinians. No. They are both groups of people who deserve to have their own country and deserve to live in peace.

But I would hope that, as we go through the testimony today, that we get to the heart of the matter. And I believe that that is the heart of the matter: The Palestinians have to agree that Israel will be able to exist and they haven't honestly done that yet.

Please feel free to contradict that in your testimony.

Mr. DESANTIS. The gentleman's time has expired.

The Chair now recognizes the gentleman from Illinois, Mr. Schneider.

Mr. SCHNEIDER. Thank you, Mr. Chair.

As we will soon hear from our witnesses, Secretary of State Kerry's efforts to broker a peace agreement between the Israelis and Palestinians took place in the context of great regional turmoil. History will determine whether or not the efforts were worth the effort.

Our challenge in the present, however, is to assess what policies we can pursue now that will help move the prospects for peace forward and, perhaps, more immediate, what policies will help ensure that the region is not moved backwards.

Much has been said lately of the decisions Israel must consider, particularly regarding borders, the security arrangements in the Jordan Valley, and prisoner releases. I believe the focus is my outlook.

Dr. Schanzer, I hope you will take the time today to elaborate on your prepared testimony on the need for Palestinians to focus, in your words, on good governance, economic reform, and institution-building.

Finally, I would like to touch briefly on the recent comments of Secretary Kerry and his reference to the specter of apartheid relative to the conflict.

As the Secretary later noted, he wished he would have used a different word. I appreciate his quick retraction and his candor.

While Israel, like any society, is not perfect, one need only look at the Arab members of the Knesset, or Salim Joubran, an Arab-Israeli judge sitting on the Supreme Court, to know that the term "apartheid" does not apply here.

The State of Israel grants full rights and security to its Arab citizens living within Israel. Full enfranchisement, full employment, full housing, and full participation in the political process are a staple of Israeli democracy.

But, more important, though unintended, the use of the word "apartheid" gives support to those who seek to delegitimize Israel and those who promote divestment and sanctions against Israel. I hope that we can count on the Secretary and others to avoid such linkage in the future.

I look forward to hearing more from our witnesses.

And I yield back the balance of my time.

Mr. DESANTIS. Gentleman yields back.

The Chair recognizes himself for 1 minute.

I want to thank the witnesses for coming. This is a very important issue and near and dear to many of our hearts.

It seems to me, especially with the unity government now with Hamas and Fatah, that the single biggest obstacle—and I will echo my colleague from California—to having a peace in this region has been a refusal to the Arabs in the region to recognize Israel as a Jewish state.

There have been multiple opportunities where you could have had a Palestinian state. The original U.N. Partition plan in the late 1940s, that was way more generous to the Arab population than to the Israelis. The Israelis accepted it. The Arabs fought it.

And, of course, we have had multiple conflicts since then. There have been multiple opportunities for there to be a true two-state solution where Israel is existing as a Jewish state.

And so, until that changes, I don't see how we are going to be able to have a resolution of this in a way that benefits Israel's security, and I do not think that we can continue in good faith to be sending U.S. taxpayer dollars over to the Palestinians if they are allied with Hamas.

I mean, Hamas—forget about recognizing Israel. I mean, they want to destroy Israel. They are not even bashful about their support of terrorism. And so I don't see how this is something that could be viewed as a positive step.

And I think we need to act in the Congress—good behavior can be rewarded, but I think you got to penalize bad behavior.

And I will now recognize the gentleman from Massachusetts, Mr. Kennedy.

Mr. KENNEDY. Thank you, Mr. Chairman. Thank you to the chairman and ranking member of the committee for calling an important hearing.

To our witnesses, thank you very much.

And to Congressman Wexler, it is great to see you again. Thank you for being here.

Gentlemen, I will be brief. I think my colleagues have framed the debate about as well as you possibly can. Just to add my voice to it, I look forward to your testimony. I look forward to the opportunity for us to ask you some questions.

I myself am particularly interested, to the extent that you can speculate, as to Abbas's decision as—to approach Hamas and the decision to reconcile, what the—prospects for a true reconciliation there actually are and what that means in the immediate term as that process continues to unfold for U.S. policy in the region.

So thank you very much again and look forward for your testimony.

Mr. DESANTIS. Gentleman yields back. And the Chair will now recognize the gentleman from California, Mr. Vargas.

Mr. VARGAS. Thank you very much, Mr. Chairman. I appreciate the opportunity.

I, too, would like to welcome the witnesses.

What I would say is that Israel has done more than any nation should have to do to try to achieve peace. They have given up their land. They have released terrorists. They have done everything they could to try to achieve peace, and the Palestinians have done nothing.

One thing I would correct for the record, I think it says Israel was born in 1948. That is modern Israel. Remember, Israel has been around since, you know, 1200 B.C. So Israel has been around for a very, very long time. Hope we recall that.

Again, I look forward to the testimony. Thank you.

Mr. DESANTIS. Want to thank the gentleman.

So I am pleased now to welcome our witnesses. Thank you for coming. Welcome back.

First, Dr. Jonathan Schanzer is vice president of research for the Foundation of Defense of Democracies. Prior to this, Dr. Schanzer served as a counterterrorism analyst at the U.S. Department of Treasury, where he took part in designating numerous terrorism financiers. So welcome.

We also have with us Mr. James Prince, who is co-founder and president of the Democracy Council. Prior to this, Mr. Prince was at PricewaterhouseCoopers, where he was engaged in the Middle East, including through an investigation of corruption at the Palestine Investment Bank.

Mr. Prince was also a senior professional staff member for this committee and helped to establish a Public Policy Institute at a university in northern Iraq.

Welcome, Mr. Prince.

And last, but certainly not least, we welcome back Mr. Robert Wexler, a former member of the Florida delegation, who is now president of the S. Daniel Abraham Center for Middle East Peace.

During his time in Congress and now at the center, Mr. Wexler has traveled extensively in the Middle East and was also chair of the Subcommittee on Europe of the House Foreign Affairs Committee and served on the Middle East Subcommittee as well.

So, welcome, Congressman Wexler.

Mr. DeSantis. At this point, I will recognize Dr. Schanzer. You guys have 5 minutes for opening statements.

And you may begin.

STATEMENT OF JONATHAN SCHANZER, PH.D., VICE PRESIDENT FOR RESEARCH, FOUNDATION FOR DEFENSE OF DEMOCRACIES

Mr. Schanzer. Mr. Chairman, Mr. Ranking Member, distinguished members of this committee, on behalf of the Foundation for Defense of Democracies, I thank you for the opportunity to discuss the recent U.S. efforts to broker peace between the Palestinians and Israelis.

I highlight four major issues of concern today.

The first is the timing of the recent initiative, particularly from Israel's perspective. The existential threat posed by Iran's nuclear program, coupled with the very serious concerns over the White House's recent decision to offer sanctions relief for a mere pause in that program, has cast a pall over every other Israeli strategic decision right now.

Of course, this threat should not stop America from pursuing peace, nor does it let the Israelis off the hook on its commitments for peacemaking. But I believe it was unrealistic to ask the Israelis to make meaningful security compromises until this crisis passes.

For that matter, it may have been unrealistic to expect the Palestinians to deliver while so many of their influential Sunni allies also express misgivings about Washington's judgment. They, too, are consumed with fear of an Iranian nuclear program.

The second area of concern is Palestinian governance. For too long, Washington has turned a blind eye to the corrupt and ossified nature of the Palestinian Authority. Given the P.A.'s 20-year track record of mishandling public funds, we might as well light a $600-million bonfire each year.

Should our assistance to the Palestinian Authority continue—and there are some good arguments for this—it must be performance-based. To be clear, this approach is both pro-Palestinian and pro-peace.

Corruption erodes the public's trust in government, and that undermines whatever deal may be reached. Conversely, a government that commands the respect of its people will earn the public's confidence to negotiate a viable solution to this conflict.

A good first step would be a plan for the departure of Mahmoud Abbas. At the age of 80, he is now 9 years into a 4-year Presidential term.

Leader for life of the Fatah faction and the PLO, Abbas crushes political opposition and silences criticism of his leadership by arresting journalists and even Facebook users. In other words, he is an autocrat.

Why our peacemakers pinned their hopes on his leadership is still unclear to me. If we want change, it is time for new leadership.

The third area of concern is the recent reconciliation agreement between the Fatah faction and Hamas. Admittedly, these two factions have tried and failed several times in the past to cement a unity deal.

There is good reason to be skeptical again. But if Hamas does join either the P.A. or the PLO, it is a sign that Islamist terror is officially welcome.

The fact that Abbas sees Hamas as even a possible partner raises troubling questions about the trajectory of the Palestinian nationalists' movement today.

Of course, a unity deal could also cause a complete rupture in U.S.- Palestinian ties. The inclusion in the Palestinian Authority of Hamas, a designated terrorist organization, is obviously a legal trigger for a full cut in funding.

Similarly, the inclusion of Hamas in the PLO might prompt a re-designation of the PLO as a terrorist organization, and that could lead to asset freezes at home and abroad.

On another note on Hamas, if we are serious about weakening this group, then pressure must be placed on two U.S. allies, Turkey and Qatar. They are among the terrorist factions' top financial and political sponsors.

How they remain allies of the United States while supporting terrorist groups—and there are others beyond Hamas—might actually be a good topic for future hearings.

Finally, I am troubled about the U.S. Government's apparent lack of readiness to confront the so-called Palestine 194 campaign.

The Palestinians have renewed their initiative at the United Nations for recognition. Never mind that the campaign is designed to spurn the U.S.-led peace process and isolate the Israelis through diplomatic lawfare.

Our laws stipulate a cut in funding to any agency that accepts the PLO. This was the case of UNESCO in 2011. Will Palestinian unilateralism prompt us to cut funding to a host of multilateral organizations?

If this is not our preferred outcome, should we not have a strategy to prevent this? If it is our preferred outcome, the process should not be predicated upon Mahmoud Abbas's diplomatic maneuvers.

In my written testimony, I note that the PLO subsidiary, the Palestine National Fund, could be funding these unilateral efforts. Some U.S. tax dollars may be allocated to the PNF through the P.A., and this could be a worthy investigation.

On behalf of FDD, I thank you again for inviting me to testify today. I look forward to your questions.

Mr. DeSantis. Thank you, Dr. Schanzer.

[The prepared statement of Mr. Schanzer follows:]

Congressional Testimony

The Palestinian Authority, Israel and the Peace Process: What's Next?

Jonathan Schanzer
Vice President for Research
Foundation for Defense of Democracies

**Hearing before the
House Committee on Foreign Affairs
Subcommittee on the Middle East and North Africa**

Washington, DC
May 8, 2014

FOUNDATION FOR
DEFENSE OF DEMOCRACIES   1726 M Street NW • Suite 700 • Washington, DC 20036

Chairman Ros-Lehtinen, Ranking Member Deutch, and distinguished members of the subcommittee, on behalf of the Foundation for Defense of Democracies, I thank you for the opportunity to discuss with you today some of the challenges associated with our recent efforts to broker peace between the Palestinians and Israelis.

After briefly reviewing Israel's security concerns during Washington's latest attempts at peacemaking, this testimony will address three specific areas of concern on the Palestinian side: Palestinian governance; Hamas-Fatah reconciliation; and the unilateral Palestinian campaign for international recognition of statehood. Finally, I provide a number of recommendations.

Israeli Defense Concerns

Secretary of State John Kerry embarked upon a bold undertaking last year, attempting to broker a peace agreement between the Palestinians and Israelis by the end of April 2014. What prompted Mr. Kerry to believe that the two sides were prepared to negotiate in good faith at this time is still unclear. True, the Palestinians and Israelis had found a *modus vivendi* that included unprecedented security cooperation[1] and an extended period of quiet. However, that was less a window for peace-making than it was a byproduct of Palestinian exhaustion after the second intifada (2000-2005), coupled with common concerns on the part of Israel and the Palestinian Authority about the rise of Hamas, which conquered the Gaza Strip in 2007.

The Israelis, while always officially open to peace talks, have in recent years been absorbed with the existential threat posed by Iran's nuclear program. The civil war in Syria, upheaval in Egypt, and the chaos of the Arab Spring have also dominated the Israeli defense agenda. This explains why the Palestinian portfolio was effectively relegated to a second tier priority. Even neutralizing the threat of Hamas rockets was pushed lower on the list of Israeli defense imperatives. As one senior Israeli official told me last year, "If they want conflict, they're going to have to get in line."

Security concerns in Israel have mounted in recent months after Washington's decision to enter into an agreement with the P5+1 and Iran that has granted Iran sanctions relief in exchange for a pause in its nuclear program. Senior Israeli officials have repeatedly and openly expressed concern that this deal will only provide Iran with more cash before it sprints to the bomb. These Israeli fears are both understandable and well founded. Iran's clerical and military leaders, despite the optimism surrounding last year's election of President Hassan Rouhani, have a long record of nuclear mendacity and an even longer record of supporting terrorist proxies, such as Hezbollah, Palestinian Islamic Jihad, and Hamas. Washington has sought to reassure the Israelis that the sanctions relief and easing isolation of Iran will not have a deleterious impact on Israeli security. To put it mildly, given Iran's history and the recent relative decline in both American hard and soft power, the Israelis are not convinced.

---

[1] Jack Khoury, Avi Issacharoff &Anshel Pfeffer, "Palestinian Authority Closely Coordinating Security Operations with Israel." *Haaretz*, January 26, 2011. www.haaretz.com/news/diplomacy-defense/palestinian-authority-closely-coordinating-security-operations-with-israel-1.339205

Amidst this ongoing crisis, the Obama administration launched the Kerry initiative. The diplomacy placed a significant amount of pressure on the Israelis to make concessions that might impact their security, even as the broader security concerns over Iran have intensified. As a result, U.S.-Israeli ties, while still strong on many levels, have been strained at the leadership level.

I should note here that these daunting security concerns do not exempt Israel from making certain compromises and concessions. It also does not give a free pass to Israel on thorny issues like settlements, which have been a somewhat consistent source of tension between the Israeli and U.S. governments. But it does explain why the Obama administration's push for Middle East peace may have been ill timed. It also may explain why Israel may not have been prepared to trust the administration's guidance -- or yield to its pressure -- at this particular point.

In short, while U.S. officials appear content to saddle Israel with the majority of the blame for the collapse of these recent talks,[2] the Iran nuclear challenge casts a shadow over all of America's interests in the Middle East. It's hard to imagine a way forward on peace without first solving this crisis.

Palestinian Governance Challenges

For all the pressure the Obama administration placed on Israel, according to press reports, there was decidedly little pressure placed on the Palestinians during this most recent drive for peace, other than asking them to refrain from returning to their international recognition campaign at the United Nations (discussed below). Of course, it can be argued that the Palestinians have less to give, since they are seeking land for their national project that is under Israeli control. But this is a myopic approach if the goal is to achieve a lasting resolution to this conflict.

In addition to making compromises on some of their core issues, Washington must ask the Palestinians to deliver on good governance, economic reform and institution building. This was glaringly absent during the most recent round of negotiations. Though seasoned professional diplomats, the Kerry team fell into a familiar trap that many of their predecessors acknowledge was a mistake. With their eyes on a deal that would yield historic handshakes on the White House lawn, they ignored the dire need to focus on the less-than-sexy task of transforming Palestinian institutions.

The fact is, America's negotiating partner on the Palestinian side – Mahmoud Abbas – is nine years into his four-year term as president of the Palestinian Authority. He also serves as leader-for-life of the PLO and the Fatah faction. He is 80 years old, a pack a day smoker, and in questionable health. Little thought has been given to what happens the day after he's gone. There is no vice president or heir apparent. In fact, there is no political structure to speak of. In other words, as American policy has backed popular Arab Spring

---

[2] Nahum Barnea, "Inside the Talks' Failure: US Officials Open Up," Ynet, May 2, 2014. www.ynetnews.com/articles/0,7340,L-4515821,00.html

movements across the Middle East, Washington placed all of its hopes for a two state solution on an autocrat.

This is not an exaggeration. Abbas has refused to hold new elections, despite his expired term, not to mention the expired term of his legislature. He refuses to allow for the creation of new political parties. He systematically crushes his political opponents.[3] Protests and unsympathetic media coverage have been met with utter brutality.[4] Denunciation of Abbas can lead to arrest.[5] In one case, gunmen fired upon the car of a Fatah leader who criticized Abbas on Facebook.[6]

To his credit, Mahmoud Abbas brought an end to the intifada in 2005, and he has made good on his promise to prevent the Fatah faction from engaging in violence. He has also made good on the security cooperation between the Palestinian security forces and the Israeli defense and intelligence establishment. But he has nevertheless emerged as a primary impediment to Palestinian political and economic advancement.

As I have noted in prior testimony, the Palestinian Authority under Abbas is not unlike how the Palestinian Authority was under Yasser Arafat – corrupt and ossified.[7] The International Crisis Group noted last year that the Palestinian Authority was suffering from "anemia," an "absence of legitimacy," and a "gradual hollowing out of institutions that were never particularly strong."[8] A recent poll reveals that more than 70 percent of Palestinians believe that nepotism is widespread in the PA.[9] As I have documented in the past, the sovereign wealth vehicle of the Palestinians also needs reform.[10] The billions of dollars in U.S. and international assistance that have poured into the Palestinian Authority over the years have served to benefit the political elite while the core infrastructure of the Palestinian Authority has stagnated. There was some cause for optimism during the years when the reformer Salam Fayyad was prime minister. But Abbas and his political allies drove out Fayyad last year, only to replace him with inexperienced bureaucrats (like new

---

[3] Stuart Winer, "Former Fatah Leader Sues 'Tyrannical' Abbas for Corruption, Intimidation," *Times of Israel*, July 24, 2013. www.timesofisrael.com/former-fatah-leader-sues-abbas-for-intimidation/
[4] See: "PA police Crush New Ramallah Demo," Ma'an News Agency, July 1, 2012. www.maannews.net/eng/ViewDetails.aspx?ID=500441; and "PA: Bethlehem Journalist Held on Criminal Charges," Ma'an News Agency, June 4, 2013. www.maannews.net/eng/ViewDetails.aspx?ID=601853
[5] Khaled Abu Toameh, "PA Police Arrest Palestinian-Canadian Investor After Calling to Oust Abbas," *Jerusalem Post*, February 12, 2013. www.jpost.com/Middle-East/PA-police-arrest-Palestinian-Canadian-investor-after-calling-to-oust-Abbas-333742
[6] "Unknown Gunmen Shoot at Fatah Leader's Car," Ma'an News Agency, July 1, 2013. www.maannews.net/eng/ViewDetails.aspx?ID=609909
[7] Jonathan Schanzer, "Chronic Kleptocracy: Corruption within the Palestinian Political Establishment," House Committee on Foreign Affairs, Subcommittee on the Middle East and South Asia, July 10, 2012. http://archives.republicans.foreignaffairs.house.gov/112/HHRG-112-FA13-WState-SchanzerJ-20120710.pdf
[8] "Buying Time? Money, Guns and Politics in the West Bank," International Crisis Group, Middle East Report No. 142, May 29, 2013. www.crisisgroup.org/en/regions/middle-east-north-africa/israel-palestine/142-buying-time-money-guns-and-politics-in-the-west-bank.aspx
[9] "Survey: Palestinians Say Nepotism Still Widespread," Associated Press, April 29, 2014. http://bigstory.ap.org/article/survey-palestinians-say-nepotism-still-widespread
[10] Omar Shaban, "Palestinian Investment Fund Needs Reform," *Al-Monitor*, May 14, 2013. www.al-monitor.com/pulse/originals/2013/05/palestinian-investment-fund-reform.html

prime minister Rami Hamdallah) and figures from Abbas' inner circle who have arguably been part of the problem (like deputy prime minister Mohammed Mustafa).

Just this February, the Palestinian Authority was embroiled in a controversy that underscores the severe lack of domestic and international trust in its management of public funds. On February 4, 2014, the Palestinian Authority adopted a budget proposal of $4.2 billion with a deficit of $1.3 billion.[11] About a week later the economic editor of the Palestinian newspaper *Al-Ayyam* published an article challenging the numbers, noting that the true current deficit was $1.889 billion -- a 49 percent deviation.[12] Shortly after that, the 2014 budget disappeared from the PA website, suggesting that the Palestinian leadership was being less than transparent. A public debate ensued, but in light of its less-than-stellar track record, many questions linger regarding the PA's fiscal responsibility.[13]

Hamas-Fatah Reconciliation

The problems of poor governance and corruption are often dismissed. But these problems have had very tangible consequences for the Palestinians. A very good case can be made that they led to the Hamas victory over Fatah in the 2006 legislative elections.

Hamas had made a name for itself over the years by carrying out spectacular acts of violence against the Israelis. But it was the Fatah faction's corruption that paved the way for Hamas' electoral win. As journalist Khaled Abu Toameh noted, there was "growing frustration on the Palestinian street as a result of mismanagement and abuse by the PLO of its monopoly on power."[14] Similarly, Bassem Eid, head of the Palestinian Human Rights Monitoring Group, noted that "everybody knows that Hamas is just climbing on such corruption of the Palestinian Authority... I think that Hamas is getting more and more supporters, while the Palestinians start in the street talking about the Palestinian corruption."[15]

In the lead-up to the January 2006 elections, Hamas hammered home that it was the clean governance ticket, accusing Fatah of corruption, nepotism, bribery, chaos, and stealing.[16] Hamas leaders promised their constituents they would battle this corruption.[17] According

---

[11] "Palestinian PM Sets $4.2bn 2014 Budget," Agence France Presse, February 4, 2014. www.google.com/hostednews/afp/article/ALeqM5iCUdLxa_yNY9wiF197Qm9gUiTCRA?docId=ef0a89df-2b17-4829-acf8-82489a779778

[12] Jafar Sadaqa, "ورقة على طاولة الحكومة: المديونة ارتفعت والعجز ضعف المقدر في الموازنة," *Al-Ayyam*, February 12, 2014. www.al-ayyam.com/pdfs/12-2-2014/p22.pdf

[13] Jafar Sadaqa, "رد الصحفي الاقتصادي جعفر صدقة على الوزارة المالية," Ma'an News Agency, February 17, 2014. www.maannews.net/Arb/ViewDetails.aspx?ID=674241

[14] Khaled Abu Toameh, "The Fallen Hope for Palestinian Press Freedom," *Jerusalem Post*, January 4, 2006. Accessed via LexisNexis.

[15] Robert Berger, "First Votes Cast in Palestinian Elections," *US Fed News – Voice of America*, January 21, 2006. Accessed via LexisNexis.

[16] Sara Toth, "Hamas TV Campaign Ad Shows Violence Aimed Symbolically at Government Corruption," Associated Press, January 22, 2006. Accessed via LexisNexis.

[17] "Hamas Calls for Palestinian Unity," Ma'an News Agency, November 1, 2005. www.maannews.net/eng/ViewDetails.aspx?ID=179066; "Hamas Announces PLC List for Tulkarem District," Ma'an News Agency, December 7, 2005.

to the Congressional Research Service, "Hamas' anti-corruption message during the parliamentary election was apparently successful, and many reports and exit polls cited anti-corruption as a motivation to vote for Hamas."[18] It didn't help that just weeks before the elections, Abbas ordered the suppression of an internal report that revealed that the Palestinian Authority had possibly lost billions of dollars as a result of financial mismanagement.[19]

This committee knows what happened next. Fatah, with backing from Israel and the United States, refused to join hands with Hamas to create a Palestinian government. This led to an internecine conflict in summer 2007, when Hamas launched a brutal military offensive in Gaza, ultimately overrunning the territory.[20] The result was a territorial and political split between the West Bank and the Gaza Strip that has endured for almost seven years.

This bloody conflict was not only a black eye for Palestinian nationalism; it has had a profound and deleterious impact on prospects for a two-state solution. Indeed, how could a solution be reached when these two Palestinian mini-states are in a state of hostility?

As it has been widely reported, the Palestinians may now be on the path to unity. The two rival factions announced a reconciliation agreement just as the Kerry diplomatic initiative collapsed.[21] As he advances in age, Abbas may view reunification as a part of his legacy. Or he may be using the agreement to pressure the Israelis. Indeed, his message seems to be that the Fatah faction and the PLO is willing to join hands with a terrorist group if he did not get the concessions he demanded of the Israelis in diplomacy.

The Fatah faction, founded as a terrorist group in the 1950s, curbed its violence against Israel during the Oslo years of the 1990s but returned to violence against Israel during the second intifada in 2000. After the death of Yasser Arafat in November 2004, Abbas brought an end to that violence in 2005. Since the internecine Palestinian conflict of 2007, security cooperation with Israel has reached an all-time high.

If there was one good thing about the Hamas-Fatah split, it was Fatah's total rejection of violent Islamist ideology, even if it was sparked by political motivations. The reconciliation deal appears to have interrupted, or even ended, this. Hamas' embrace of

---

www.maannews.net/eng/ViewDetails.aspx?ID=180294; "Hamas Leader Hania Lays Out Elections Agenda, Including Three Points," Ma'an News Agency, December 9, 2005.
www.maannews.net/eng/ViewDetails.aspx?ID=180394; and "Hamas to Enter Qassam Brigades Into PA Security Forces, End 'Bombing Operations,'" Ma'an News Agency, December 19, 2005.
www.maannews.net/eng/ViewDetails.aspx?ID=180783.
[18] Aaron Pina, "Palestine Elections," Congressional Research Service, February 9, 2006. www.fas.org/sgp/crs/mideast/RL33269.pdf.
[19] Chris McGreal, "Palestinian Authority 'May Have Lost Billions'," *The Guardian*, February 5, 2006. www.guardian.co.uk/world/2006/feb/06/israel.
[20] Steven Erlanger, "Hamas Seizes Broad Control in Gaza Strip," *New York Times*, June 14, 2007. www.nytimes.com/2007/06/14/world/middleeast/14midcast.html?_r=1&
[21] Kareem Khadder & Jason Hanna, "Hamas, Fatah Announce Talks to Form Palestinian Unity Government," CNN.com, April 23, 2014. www.cnn.com/2014/04/23/world/meast/gaza-west-bank-palestinian-reconciliation/

terrorism is full-throated, and so is its rejection of Israel. Hamas has already made it clear that it will not disarm or alter its violent ideology any time soon.[22] Reports this week now indicate that Palestinian security forces, trained by the U.S. and armed by our Arab allies, may now integrate with Hamas forces in Gaza.[23]

Of course, these two political foes have attempted to reconcile several times in the past and failed. But the timing of this recent deal -- on the heels of a collapse in U.S.-sponsored talks -- may indicate a new seriousness of purpose. The two sides met earlier this week in Qatar with the emir, Sheikh Tamim,[24] who has already reportedly agreed to pay $5 million to "families who lost relatives to infighting between Fatah and Hamas."[25] Qatar could be asked to bear the financial burdens of underwriting a unity government–particularly if part or all of Washington's $600 million in funding is cut by Congress, and the estimated $100 million per month in Value Added Tax (VAT) is withheld by Israel.

Proponents of this most recent reconciliation agreement insist that the next step is not a unity government, but rather a technocratic government that would include apolitical figures selected by both parties. As Israel's ambassador to Washington recently noted, Israel does not accept this distinction.[26] And it is unlikely that Congress will, either.

That's where countries like Qatar come in. Abbas has also appealed to the Arab League for funds.[27] Other countries, such as Turkey, may also be willing to make up for financial shortfalls, if the upshot is a Hamas-Fatah unity government.[28] Turkey has already been suspected of providing direct assistance to Hamas since 2011, when several news outlets reported that the government of Recep Tayyip Erdoğan allocated some $300 million.[29]

---

[22] "Hamas Official Says Security Services to Stay in Place Until After Election," *Middle East Monitor*, May 2, 2014. www.middleeastmonitor.com/news/middle-east/11231-hamas-official-says-security-services-to-stay-in-place-until-after-election; and Crispian Balmer & Nidal al-Mughrabi, "Palestinian Deal Will Not Make Hamas Change: Veteran Leader," Reuters, April 29, 2014. www.reuters.com/article/2014/04/29/us-palestinian-israel-hamas-idUSBREA3S0LD20140429

[23] "3,000 PA Officers 'to Join Gaza Security Forces' in Unity Step," Ma'an News Agency, May 5, 2014. www.maannews.net/eng/ViewDetails.aspx?ID=694901

[24] "Abbas, Hamas Chief to Hold First Talks Since Unity Deal," Agence France Presse, May 5, 2014. www.hurriyetdailynews.com/abbas-hamas-chief-to-hold-first-talks-since-unity-deal.aspx?pageID=238&nID=65979&NewsCatID=352

[25] "Qatar Looks to Mend Hamas-Fatah Ties with $5 Million Pledge," *Jerusalem Post*, May 5, 2014. www.jpost.com/Middle-East/Qatar-looks-to-mend-Hamas-Fatah-ties-with-5-million-pledge-351341

[26] "A Conversation with Ron Dermer," Foundation for Defense of Democracies, Washington Forum, May 1, 2014. www.fddnews.com/transcript.html?item=20140501t2691&op=nw&addr=NW1-DF1-ME1-FO1-HS1-BB1

[27] Jack Khoury, "Fearing Israeli Sanctions, Abbas to Ask Arab League for Economic Aid," *Haaretz*, April 8, 2014. www.haaretz.com/news/diplomacy-defense/.premium-1.584472

[28] "Turkey Welcomes Deal Between Palestine's Hamas, Fatah," Anadolu Agency, April 24, 2014. www.aa.com.tr/en/news/317818--turkey-welcomes-deal-between-palestines-hamas-fatah

[29] See: Saed Bannoura, "Turkey to Grant Hamas $300 Million," *International Middle East Media Center*, December 3, 2011. www.imemc.org/article/62607; Nidal al-Mughrabi, "Hamas Quietly Quits Syria as Violence Continues," Reuters, January 27, 2012. www.reuters.com/article/2012/01/27/us-syria-hamas-idUSTRE80Q0QS20120127; and Zvi Bar'el, "Turkey May Provide Hamas with $300 Million in Annual Aid," *Haaretz*, January 28, 2012. www.haaretz.com/news/diplomacy-defense/turkey-may-provide-hamas-with-300-million-in-annual-aid-1.409708

Turkey has also been providing Hamas with assistance for hospitals,[30] mosques,[31] schools,[32] food supplies,[33] and energy.[34]

Palestine 194

Ironically, the Palestinian leadership's flirtation with an internationally-condemned terrorist organization also coincides with the resumption of a unilateral campaign for international recognition.

On April 1, the Palestinians announced that Abbas had signed letters of accession to 15 multilateral treaties and conventions.[35] Last week, the Palestinians also announced that they had become signatories to five of those conventions,[36] with plans to sign some 60 others.[37]

The campaign is not new. Abbas initiated it nine years ago, in 2005. "Palestine 194," as it is known in PLO circles, is designed to circumvent bilateral negotiations with Israel and gain Palestinian recognition on the world stage. Apart from its rejection of diplomacy, the campaign effectively asks the international community to ignore the many shortfalls of Palestinian governance mentioned above. Finally, leveraging the widespread sympathy for the Palestinian cause in the United Nations, the campaign is intended to spark wide opprobrium of Israel in a wide range of agencies.

For more than five years, the Palestinians quietly laid the groundwork for the campaign, and purportedly found support from 128 countries.[38] Then, in the wake of a failed settlement freeze in 2010, Abbas responded with a dramatic declaration of state at the United Nations in 2011.[39] The move was rebuffed by the United States, thanks to its veto power at the Security Council, which alone holds the power to formally acknowledge

---

[30] "Turkey Building Hospital in Gaza Despite Difficulties," *Today's Zaman*, July 19, 2011. www.todayszaman.com/news-250982-turkey-building-hospital-in-gaza-despite-difficulties.html

[31] "Turkey to Help Rebuild Mosques in Gaza Strip," *Hurriyet Daily News*, January 12, 2012. www.hurriyetdailynews.com/turkey-to-help-rebuild-mosques-in-gaza-strip.aspx?pageID=238&nID=11286&NewsCatID=338%29

[32] "Gaza Govt Constructs, Refurbishes 50 Security Buildings," Ma'an News Agency, January 24, 2012. www.maannews.net/eng/ViewDetails.aspx?ID=454664

[33] Elad Benari, "Israel Allows Turkish Food Trucks into Gaza," *Arutz Sheva*, March 7, 2013. www.israelnationalnews.com/News/News.aspx/165959#.Uml2aPmshsI

[34] "Turkey Donates $850,000 For Gaza's Energy Needs," *Today's Zaman*, October 23, 2013. www.todayszaman.com/news-329599-turkey-donates-850000-for-gazas-energy-needs.html

[35] "Ministry of Foreign Affairs Files Applications to Join International Treaties," Palestinian News and Information Agency (WAFA), April 2, 2014. www.wafa.ps/english/index.php?action=detail&id=24782

[36] "Palestinians Become Signatories in 5 UN Human Rights Conventions," Agence France Presse, May 2, 2014. www.ynetnews.com/articles/0,7340,L-4515765,00.html

[37] Jack Khoury, "PLO Votes to Sign Palestine Up for 63 UN Accords—Abbas to Decide When," *Haaretz*, April 28, 2014. www.haaretz.com/news/diplomacy-defense/.premium-1.587759

[38] "Palestine's Application for UN Membership," PLO Negotiations Affairs Department, October 2011. www.nad-plo.org/etemplate.php?id=303

[39] "Full transcript of Abbas speech at UN General Assembly," *Haaretz*, September 23, 2011. www.haaretz.com/news/diplomacy-defense/full-transcript-of-abbas-speech-at-un-general-assembly-1.386385

new states. Led by efforts in the U.S. Congress, Washington also withheld $200 million in financial assistance as a warning to the Palestinians not to return to the UN.[40]

But Abbas was not deterred. He soon made a play for membership at the United Nations Educational, Scientific and Cultural Organization (UNESCO). The vote took place on October 2011, with 107 of 173 countries voting in favor.[41] Congress then slashed its support for UNESCO, too. According to a little-known American law from the 1990s, the U.S. is prohibited from giving funds to any part of the UN system that grants the PLO the same standing as member states.[42]

Despite these setbacks, by early 2012 the PLO signaled that it was poised for another run at the UN – but this time at the General Assembly. After a number of fits and starts, the Palestinians settled on November 29, a day that followed the U.S. elections, so as to not infuriate President Barack Obama, who had been adamantly opposed to the initiative. It was also the anniversary of the 1947 U.N. partition plan, which allocated territory to both Jews and Arabs. In the end, 138 countries voted in favor of the initiative. Only 9 voted against—eight, not including Israel. To be clear, the vote was only symbolic. The General Assembly does not have the authority to make the State of Palestine the 194th member country of the United Nations.

In short, the Palestinians demonstrated that their campaign could not be derailed. Not even the United States could prevent their bid for recognition. This, in part, explains the urgency of the Obama administration's new peace process, launched in the spring of 2013. While the administration put significant pressure on the Israelis to make concessions on borders, Jerusalem, and settlements, perhaps the only major demand on the Palestinians was to halt Palestine 194.

The Palestinians cooled their heels, but they also continued to study steps to join UN treaties and bodies, and often threatened to return to the campaign.[43] Palestinian official Hanan Ashrawi, for example, warned that the Palestinian leadership was ready to join sixteen agencies beginning in April 2014, at the end of the diplomatic window stipulated by the Obama administration.[44] In late December, Palestinian negotiator Saeb Erekat

---

[40] Natasha Mozgovaya, "U.S. Congress Officially Confirms Blocking Palestinian Aid, Explains Reasoning," *Haaretz*, October 4, 2011. www.haaretz.com/news/diplomacy-defense/u-s-congress-officially-confirms-blocking-palestinian-aid-explains-reasoning-1.387989

[41] "Palestinians Get UNESCO Seat as 107 Vote in Favour," BBC.com, October 31, 2011. www.bbc.com/news/world-middle-east-15518173

[42] Title 22, Section 287e of the U.S. Code prohibits U.S. funding to (1) "the United Nations or any specialized agency thereof which accords the Palestine Liberation Organization the same standing as member states," and (2) to the UN or "to any affiliated organization of the United Nations which grants full membership as a state to any organization or group that does not have the internationally recognized attributes of statehood." They were enacted, respectively, as Public Law 101-246 in 1990 and Public Law 103-236 in 1994. See www.gpo.gov/fdsys/pkg/USCODE-2009-title22/html/USCODE-2009-title22-chap7-subchapXVI-sec287e.htm and http://uscode.house.gov/statutes/1994/1994-103-0236.pdf

[43] "PLO Studies Steps to Join UN Treaties, Bodies," Ma'an News Agency, January 3, 2013. www.maannews.net/eng/ViewDetails.aspx?ID=553276

[44] Catherine Philp, "Palestinians Plan UN Move to Show Up Washington," *The Times* (UK), December 2 2013. www.thetimes.co.uk/tto/news/world/middleeast/article3937380.ece

announced that there were no less than sixty-three member agencies of the UN that the PLO sought to join.[45] Last month, the Palestinian ambassador to the UN claimed that 550 agencies and conventions were fair game.[46] Senior Palestinian official Nabil Shaath warned that the Palestinians could use the "weapon" of taking claims against Israel to the International Criminal Court.[47]

Israeli officials quietly admit that the ICC is only one agency on a short list of international bodies that they view as red lines. They include the International Telecommunications Union (ITU), the International Civil Aviation Organization (ICAO), the International Maritime Organization (IMO), the World Trade Organization (WTO) and INTERPOL. The concern for Israel is that, not only would the Palestinians gain acceptance as a state (and do so outside of the bilateral peace process), but that they would also seek to isolate Israel from these agencies, which are vital for Israeli commerce, security, or diplomacy.[48]

The Palestine 194 campaign is not only a concern for Israel. It could also harm U.S. interests, in light of the fact that our laws could prompt a cut in funding to any agency that accepts Palestinian membership. While State Department officials have acknowledged this concern to me, it is unclear whether the U.S. government is in any way prepared for the isolation that could result from this campaign once it gets underway.

Recommendations

In light of the above challenges, I respectfully submit the following recommendations.

1. **Stop Iran from getting the bomb, and soon.** The longer this crisis lingers, the longer it will cast doubt on America's ability to impose its will in the Middle East. As long as the climate of fear persists, the Israelis will be less likely to make concessions that impact their security. Similarly, Sunni Arab states like Saudi Arabia will be less inclined to push the Palestinians to the table. Put simply, the Iran nuclear challenge overshadows everything else in the region.

2. **Condition Palestinian aid on transparency and good governance.** Aid should not be based solely on supporting the peace process, as it has been until now. Aid needs to be conditional and performance-based. We need to keep expectations high.

3. **Require that Palestinian economic development be based on sustainable practices, not political patronage.** Selection of partners for business opportunities

---

[45] "عريقات: سنتوجه لـ63 منظمة دولية في حال طرح عطاءات استيطانية جديدة" Ma'an News Agency, December 26, 2013. www.maannews.net/arb/ViewDetails.aspx?ID=660471

[46] "Ambassador: Palestine Eligible for 550 Intl Orgs," Ma'an News Agency, April 2, 2014. www.maannews.net/eng/ViewDetails.aspx?ID=687069%20

[47] "Shaath: Palestine Prepared to Join More UN Orgs," Ma'an News Agency, November 26, 2013. www.maannews.net/eng/ViewDetails.aspx?ID=651372

[48] First reported in: Jonathan Schanzer & Grant Rumley, "Palestine's Plan for When Peace Talks Fail," *The National Interest*, March 17, 2014. http://nationalinterest.org/commentary/palestines-plan-when-peace-talks-fail-10061

must be a completely objective process where the best and most transparent companies are awarded contracts. This cannot be tainted by political objectives. Too much nepotism, waste, and corruption has already eroded Palestinian growth.

4. **Take the "peace processors" away from the economic process.** Economic development must be left to the economists. Too many sweetheart deals were cut during the heyday of the peace process. The prevailing thinking appeared to be that, if the most important Palestinians were sated by lucrative business deals, they would not have the stomach to engage again in hostilities. That thinking was wrong. Not only did the peace process unravel, but the Palestinian economy collapsed.

5. **The old guard must go.** Washington must pave the way for the orderly exit of Mahmoud Abbas and his clique. After a decade of corruption and poor governance, new parties and new leaders must be given an opportunity to emerge. Indeed, the Palestinians need a marketplace of ideas if there is to be change. Right now, political challengers are crushed. This portends poorly for the future of the system and could ultimately enable Hamas to seize power in the event of a leadership crisis.

6. **Prevent Hamas from joining the Palestinian Authority and/or the PLO.** Reconciliation is not yet a done deal. Washington must make it clear that all funding will be slashed should Hamas become part of a national unity government or even a technocratic government approved by Hamas. This is a matter of enforcing existing U.S. law. Similarly, the PLO must understand that it can be placed under U.S. sanctions should it allow Hamas to join its ranks. Hamas will deal a blow to any future chance at diplomacy.

7. **Put more pressure on Hamas' regional supporters.** Turkey and Qatar are two U.S. allies and two of Hamas' strongest backers. These countries could determine the future success or failure of a unity government. They must be convinced to cease their political and financial support to Hamas. As Secretary of State John Kerry stated in 2009 when he was U.S. senator, "Qatar... cannot continue to be an American ally on Monday that sends money to Hamas on Tuesday."[49] The same goes for Turkey.

8. **Counter the Palestine 194 Campaign.** Washington must move quickly before the Palestinian international recognition campaign prompts additional cut-offs at UN agencies, like the one prompted by the PLO accession to UNESCO. While the United Nations is highly dysfunctional and often harmful to American interests, some agencies are of value. Cuts in funding should be strategic, and not dictated by Palestinian maneuverings. While communication is already well established, Washington must engage with the relevant agencies to see what solutions are available. Congress may also begin to identify legal mechanisms to challenge this campaign.

---

[49] John Kerry, "Restoring Leadership in the Middle East: A Regional Approach to Peace," Remarks at the Brookings Institution, March 4, 2009.
www.brookings.edu/~/media/Events/2009/3/04%20leadership/0304_leadership.PDF

9. **Investigate the PNF**. The Palestine National Fund receives funding from the Palestinian Authority budget, to which America contributes some 20 percent annually.[50] The PNF is often viewed as the main financial body of the PLO.[51] The PNF has in the past used its funds to "to help families of 'martyrs,' and to educate refugees, as well as funding Palestinian media organs."[52] Today, it provides funding to PLO missions around the world.[53] Those missions have been responsible for lobbying on behalf of the Palestine 194 initiative. Congress should determine whether the U.S. directly or indirectly funds the PNF, and take action accordingly.

On behalf of the Foundation for Defense of Democracies, I thank you again for inviting me to testify before this distinguished committee.

---

[50] "PA 2013 Draft Budget Excludes Fuel Revenues," Ma'an News Agency, April 6, 2013. www.maannews.net/eng/ViewDetails.aspx?ID=576647

[51] "Palestine Liberation Organization (PLO)," Embassy of the State of Palestine in Malaysia, www.palestineembassy.org/plo.html

[52] "Jawed al-Ghussein: PLO Treasurer Kidnapped by Arafat," *The Independent*, August 27, 2008. www.independent.co.uk/news/obituaries/jawed-alghussein-plo-treasurer-kidnapped-by-arafat-909610.html

[53] "Abbas Appoints Ramzi Khoury as Director of the Palestine National Fund," *Al Jazeera*, April 27, 2005. www.aljazeera.net/ebusiness/pages/75f07b90-8c5d-46c0-8d30-d49b2e8ed000

Mr. DeSantis. And the Chair now recognizes Mr. Prince for 5 minutes.

STATEMENT OF MR. JAMES PRINCE, CO-FOUNDER AND PRESIDENT, THE DEMOCRACY COUNCIL

Mr. Prince. Thank you, Mr. Chairman, Mr. Ranking member.

Despite the essential conditions for peace existing on both sides, as distinguished members of this subcommittee noted, in Secretary Kerry's Herculean efforts, the diplomatic effort has failed again.

I will confine my comments to the Palestinian side of this equation. It is not meant to ignore or diminish the unique and tremendous hardships posed by the occupation, but, rather, to discuss the imperative of dealing with the internal dynamics and the corruption inherent in the Palestinian Authority.

Since the establishment of the Palestinian Authority, the U.S. has vacillated in its attention to internal Palestinian politics. Criticism of the P.A. leadership was often perceived as a distraction or detrimental to the peace process. The immediate need of support in peace negotiation often pushed issues of fostering good governance, civil society to a second tier.

Taking risks necessary to achieve peace and enhance the quality of life in Palestine requires leaders with not only the courage, but, also, a political mandate that will support such risk-taking.

Even within Mr. Abbas's inner circle, there is a consensus that Mr. Abbas does not feel he has the political mandate to take such risks, and he is not strong enough to support any negotiated agreement that he negotiates.

The Abbas P.A. has become a single-party police state ruled by Presidential decree. Debate and criticism is not tolerated. Corruption and nepotism has washed away much of the goodwill and legitimacy conferred onto the regime after Abbas succeeded Arafat.

The absence of national elections following the expiration of the Presidential term in 2009 further degrades the legitimacy of the P.A. in the eyes of its own constituents.

Abbas is likely to retire in advance of the next election. This will signal an abrupt end to the Arafat era and older generation.

Infighting within the Fatah Central Committee has so far precluded emergence of a consensus legacy candidate. Polls indicate the Fatah would still win over 40 percent of the vote, with Hamas receiving upwards of 12 percent.

The most remarkable indicator that should be noted is that 34 percent of the eligible voters in the West Bank and Gaza are undecided or just don't agree with any of the current leadership.

Allegations of corruption and mismanagement have plagued the P.A. since its inception. In 1999, I helped manage an investigation into the Palestinian International Bank.

We presented Yasser Arafat with massive evidence of fraud, mismanagement, and illegalities. We suggested to him that he take the report and pass it over to the appropriate law enforcement officials.

He replied, in very characteristic candor, ''Why? The Palestinian people trust me more than they trust the Palestinian Authority or any institution.'' President Abbas has taken this rule by Presidential decree to a whole other level.

The so-called Fayyadism and a focus on institution-building not only reduced corruption, but, importantly, stimulated government collections, in spite of a decrease in gross domestic product.

For the first time during Salam Fayyad's previous tenure as finance minister, the Palestinian budget received applause.

I participated in a worldwide investigation that brought back over $700 billion into the Treasury and helped eliminate much of the pervasive smuggling and corruption. However, this very intermittent, positive trend ended following the 2006 election.

The international response was to wall off the Ramallah from the Gaza Strip. The temporary international mechanism followed by the Pegasus system not only channeled cash assistance and succeeded in stabilizing the P.A., but it reinvigorated an Imperial presidency that Abbas has continued to this day.

Except for select ministries and agencies, such as the Palestinian Monetary Authority and Ministry of Education, few government offices operate to international standards. The Palestinian Investment Fund is one of the most controversial tools used by Abbas to wield influence and direct favors.

As previous testimony to the subcommittee indicates, beginning in 2007, the PIF has operated largely as an extension of the presidency, directed by the chairman and CEO of the fund, who happens also to be deputy prime minister.

In violation of its own charter, the PIF often directly competes against the local businesses and has a way of garnering favors with the leadership.

In my written testimony, I talk about the Hamas and Fatah reconciliation and the challenges it posed. U.S. Law regarding cutting off assistance to a government that includes Hamas and the Quartet Principles for recognition are clear. Without workarounds, this drastic measure should only be deployed as a last resort.

I would like to skip to some of the suggestions for USG programming that I included in my written testimony. They include avoiding large economic projects controlled by the Authority, gearing more toward small business in the West Bank and Gaza, with an emphasis on underserved communities.

We should devote additional funding for rule-of-law programming. We need to dedicate additional resources to fostering independent life, political party development, independent candidate training, and independent need, as to avoid some of the missteps done by USAID and other international organizations in preparation for the 2006 elections.

U.S. Government assistance should also include evidence of institutional reform, such as a participatory election law that precludes candidates that advocate violence, civil service and pension reform, adding an office of Vice President, and allowing the P.A. ministers the ability to appoint their own deputies and department heads without Presidential interference.

The Palestinian Authority remains the best vehicle by which to bring about durable peace in the region. However, lacking a political mandate from its own constituency, the P.A. leadership will be unable and unwilling to make the difficult decisions needed to move from the status quo.

Thank you again for this opportunity.

Mr. DeSantis. Thank the gentleman.
[The prepared statement of Mr. Prince follows:]

28

TESTIMONY OF

JAMES PRINCE

THE DEMOCRACY COUNCIL

BEFORE THE

SUBCOMMITEEE ON MIDDLE EAST & NORTH AFRICA

OF THE

HOUSE FOREIGN AFFAIRS COMMITTEE

ON

THE PALESTINIAN AUTHORITY, ISRAEL AND THE PEACE PROCESS:
WHERE DO WE GO FROM HERE?

MARCH 8, 2014

Chairman Ros-Lehtinen, Ranking Member Deutsch, and distinguished members of the Subcommittee on Middle East and North Africa, I would like to thank you for holding this hearing today and inviting me to testify on "*The Palestinian Authority, Israel and the Peace Process: Where do we go from here*". With your approval, I would like to submit my written testimony for the record.

I base my testimony on five years of working as a consultant to the Palestinian Authority, and thirteen years as President of the Democracy Council working in the Middle East & North Africa region.

This hearing comes on the heels of another unsuccessful effort to reach a final status agreement between Israelis and Palestinians. Despite the essential conditions for peace existing on both sides and Secretary Kerry's herculean efforts, the diplomatic effort has stalled again. The PA responded with a renewed effort to pursue further recognition with the United Nations, and to reconcile with Hamas.

I have been asked to discuss the internal dynamics and political trends within the Palestinian Authority. For the purposes of this hearing, I will confine my comments to the "Palestinian side" and not discuss or assign blame for the latest breakdown in negotiations. That being said, I do not mean to ignore or diminish the unique and tremendous hardships and severe impact of the Israeli occupation and settlement construction in any way. As Secretary Kerry emphasizes, solving the Palestinian – Israeli conflict based upon a two-state solution requires hard choices with tangible investments in peace by both sides.

Since the establishment of the Palestinian Authority, the United States has vacillated in its attention to internal Palestinian politics. Except for the 2002 to 2004 period, our policy toward internal Palestinian affairs has focused on (1) Fighting terror and marginalizing terrorist groups, and (2) Fostering support for the Oslo peace process. Criticism of the PA leadership was often perceived as distraction or detrimental to the peace process. The immediate need of supporting peace negotiations often pushed issues of fostering good governance, political life, and an active civil society to a lower priority.

Yet not recognizing, and dealing with, the rampant corruption, mismanagement and increasing delegitimization of the PA's leadership in the eyes of its own constituents, has done a disservice to the Palestinians. Taking risks necessary to achieve a durable peace and enhance the quality of life in the West Bank and Gaza requires leaders with not only political courage but also a real or obtainable political mandate from a core constituency that would support such risk-taking. Many of President and Chairman of the Palestine Liberation Organization (PLO) Mahmoud Abbas' (Abu Mazen) own advisors have concluded that regardless a personal inclination to make peace, Abbas feels that he does not have such a mandate from his Fatah base in the West Bank, while Hamas in Gaza would, in his opinion, effectively torpedo the implementation of any deal negotiated without them.

CORRUPTION & CONSOLIDATION OF POWER

The Abbas – PA has become a single – party police state ruled by Presidential decree in which corruption and coercion dominate most aspects of life in the West Bank. Internal debate or criticism is not tolerated. Limiting political activity to only the top echelons of Fatah, quashing dissent, increasing corruption and nepotism has washed away much of the good will and legitimacy conferred onto the regime after Abbas succeeded Arafat as president and chairman. The absence of national elections following the expiration of the current presidential term in January, 2009, further degrades the legitimacy of the PA in the eyes of its own constituents. Most Palestinians in both the West Bank and Gaza believe that a presidential election is critical to restoring a degree of legitimacy to the PA.[1] Elections do, however, contain attendant risks, as illustrated by the 2006 parliamentary elections in which Hamas emerged victorious, and the recent experience in Egypt. Local extremist groups would no doubt gain some grassroots support by showcasing what plays locally as Israel's retreat from the spirit of Oslo, especially its settlement expansion, as well as the issue of corruption within the PA.

Abbas is likely to retire in advance of the next election. Infighting within the Fatah central committee has so far precluded emergence of a consensus legacy candidate. Meanwhile, a significant portion of the population sees the older generation of Fatah leaders, such as Abbas, as increasingly out of touch, lacking the skills to govern and manage relations with Israel. This feeling of marginalization and voter apathy led to younger "independent" candidates beating out traditional Fatah candidates in six of the eleven districts during the October 2012 local elections.

According to a recent poll by the Arab World for Research and Development, "if national elections were held today, a Fatah electoral list would receive 42 percent of votes, and a Hamas list would receive 12 percent. 34% would not vote are undecided." (This high level of voter apathy for the two main parties could bode well for a popular reform movement that is able to freely campaign and effectively distinguish itself from the existing leadership.)

Allegation of corruption, mismanagement, nepotism and authoritarian rule has plagued the PA since its inception. In 1999, I helped manage an investigation of the Palestine International Bank. We presented then-President Yasser Arafat evidence of fraud, corruption, and mismanagement, recommending that the report be referred to appropriate law enforcement offices in anticipation of a public prosecution in accordance with Palestinian law and international standards. Arafat replied that a public prosecution would be unnecessarily messy given that (1) the public trusted him to make the correct decision, and (2) the Palestinian justice system could not remain immune from the political pressures involved with such a high profile trial. Arafat simply issued a Presidential decree assuming control of the bank. Except for a brief period of reform ushered in during Salam Fayyad's tenure as Finance Minister, in which the

---

[1] Arab World for Research and Development, *National Opinion Poll*, April 1, 2014
http://www.awrad.org/page.php?id=cEhtq9M4DCa9852360AKQBuvzxIbp

Palestine Legislative Council met on a regular basis, this type of Presidential rule by decree serves as the primary political activity in the PA.

In June 2002, President Bush announced unequivocal support for an independent Palestinian state while calling for new Palestinian leadership dedicated to building a "practicing democracy, built on tolerance and liberty. True reform will require entirely new political and economic institutions, based on democracy, market economics and action against terrorism." President Bush called attention to the fact that the Palestinian legislature and local officials had no real authority.[2] The next few years saw substantial progress. So called "Fayyadism" and a focus on institution building, not only drastically reduced corruption but importantly stimulated government collections in spite of a decrease in GDP. The reformers began the difficult process of moving the focus of the narrative away from that of only "resistance against Israel," and political posturing toward improving life in Palestine, despite the hardships of occupation, in preparation for an independent state. There was recognition that the old style of an autocratic presidential model, like those of Egypt or Syria, needs to be replaced by a more accountable executive with counterbalanced powers in the legislative and judicial branches.

Initially, then - Finance Minister Fayyad received international support to institute reforms requisite for a viable public administration in a new independent state. The United States Government and donor community refocused significant diplomatic and programmatic efforts aimed at decentralizing power and weakening the imperial presidency with tangible results. For the first time, the Palestinian budget received applause for its integrity. Nebulous and secretive armed militias were incorporated into the national security forces. I participated in a worldwide investigation of over $1 billion of revenue generating assets that brought back over $700 million into the Palestinian treasury and helped eliminate much of the pervasive smuggling and corruption. In 2003, we helped design the Palestine Investment Fund whose aims were to remove the President from continue to intrude into the private sector at his whim, and to launch a transparent, publically accountable means of managing the PA's intervention into the local economy. Just as importantly, Palestinian civil society began to organize and advocate on its own behalf.

The positive trend ended following the 2006 parliamentary elections and the resultant splitting of the administration of the West Bank and Gaza. The international response was to politically wall-off the Hamas-controlled Gaza strip from the interim government in Ramallah. The U.S. supported a direct assistance mechanism, Temporary International Mechanism (TIM), administered by the European Union (EU), which provided direct cash assistance through the office of President Mahmoud Abbas. Originally envisioned as a three-month emergency mechanism, the TIM system was morphed into the much larger PEGASE system in February 2008. Although this massive direct financial support can be credited with averting a

---

[2] "President Bush Calls for new Palestinian Leadership, June 24, 2002 http://georgewbush-whitehouse.archives.gov/news/releases/2002/06/20020624-3.html

humanitarian disaster and keeping the PA afloat, it also resulted in reviving the imperial presidency that bypassed institutional processes and rule of law or bureaucratic checks and balances. This system continues to flourish today.

While progress has been made in PA budgeting and planning, the civil service remains grossly inflated with plum civil service jobs, some real, some not, gifted as rewards by the executive for political acquiescence. A 2013 internal EU audit reinforced the widespread perception that the PEGASE program subsidizes a grossly inflated civil service payroll in the West Bank and ghost employees in Gaza. [3] The government payroll serves, to a degree, as a means of garnering support for the PA political leadership. (Approximately 170,000 Palestinians and their families are beholden to the PA for their salaries and pensions.)

The Abbas presidency steadily consolidated political and economic power while decimating civil society activity. Except for select ministries and agencies, such as the Palestinian Monetary Authority and Ministry of Education, few government offices function to international standards. Fatah and old-time PLO loyalists dominate all aspects of political life in the West Bank. Using the one party-system to his advantage, Abbas effectively marginalized Fayyad and the new generation of reformers who dared to rear their head above the parapet after Arafat's death. Dissent is summarily squashed. A former Minister said as recently as last week that there is evidence that the President's office ordered widespread wire-tapping of not only critics and journalists but also PA officials.

The defunct legislature prevents a separation of powers and limits oversight mechanisms. The judiciary and internal security forces are perceived as a tool wielded arbitrarily by the President and his close cohorts. As the former Minister recently stated, Palestine and Syria may be the last remaining "presidential police states" in the Arab world.

The United Nations and independent NGOs continue to report that Palestinians are subject to a wide range of human rights violations not only in relation to the Israel Defense Forces but from the PA security services. The special corruption court and the judiciary in general are known for their subjective and overly politicized investigations prosecuting those who refuse to offer "waste" to the Fatah leadership. Efforts by civil society organizations on behalf of vulnerable groups is challenged by interference from security agencies.

Intimidation and arbitrary arrests of independent journalists or reporters known to collaborate with international press have been well documented. Investigative reporting or calls for transparency result in arrests and harassment. Judges report receiving calls "suggesting" decisions and prosecutions that benefit Abbas. Similarly, bank officials complain of pressure from the PA leadership to promote commercial and protect businesses that support Abbas.

---

[3] European Court of Auditors, *European Union Direct Financial Support to the Palestinian Authority*, Special Report No. 13, 2013 http://www.eca.europa.eu/Lists/ECADocuments/SR13_14/SR13_14_EN.pdf

PALESTINE INVESTMENT FUND

Nowhere is the consolidation of power more prevalent than in the economy. Top-down nepotism runs rampant in the West Bank. Sweetheart deals, concessions, and permitting not only limit opportunity for the average Palestinian but serve as a vehicle to demand political support. The Palestinian Investment Fund (PIF) is one of the most obvious and controversial tools used by Abbas to wield influence and direct favors.

The stated purpose of the PIF included decentralizing presidential power and removing the executive from being able to arbitrarily intrude into the private sector. The public fund was established as a transparent, independently managed sovereign wealth fund by which to conduct economic stimulus programs in distressed private sectors. And from 2003 to 2006, the PIF ended or sold off tens of schemes and enterprises that did not meet international standards and/or were inappropriate for a public investment. Hundreds of millions of dollars were brought back into the Palestinian treasury. The policies and procedures governing the fund's operations restricted investment activity to assuming risk in distressed private sectors that would not compete with local business and be mutually exclusive from political expediencies and political whims.

As previous testimony to this subcommittee indicates, however, beginning in 2007 the PIF has largely operated as an extension of the Presidency, a tool by which to curry favors, lavish gifts, and marginalize critics. Despite the original conflict of interest restriction, the PIF's current Chairman & Chief Executive Officer, Muhammad Mustafa, not only serves on many private sector boards of directors but is also the appointed Deputy Prime Minister. In fact, many in the Cabinet reportedly refer to Mustafa, rather than the prime minister, as the "boss."

Under the rubric of creating jobs, the PIF serves as an economic powerbroker. Increasingly, the Fund is viewed by average Palestinians as epitomizing the corruption associated with the intertwining of power, politics and business. By any calculation, the PIF and its individual board of directors, appointed by the President in contradiction to the original operating policies, control most aspects of economic activity in the West Bank. Businessmen report that in order to conduct business or access local financial services or regulatory offices they must pay homage to either the PIF or directly to the President. Calls for the PIF to release its outside auditor's working papers and notes continue to be ignored, despite the fact that the fund exists as a public fund.

In violation of its own charter, the PIF often competes directly against local businesses. For example, in 2009, the PIF beat out private sector competitors to obtain a controversial license for a new cell phone company combined with publicly-backed bank loans to support the launch of the mobile network. It was not lost on the Palestinian public that Fayyad had earlier forced the PIF to sell off its investments in the cell phone sector, stating that it was unfair competition with the private sector. Now, government employees and those seeking to do business with the PA report pressure to use the new Wataniyya mobile network. I recently heard details about how a prominent businessman had to make a $1.5 million "contribution" to the President's operating budget and guarantee subcontracts to the PIF in order to obtain building and land-use permits. Those in the private sector also point to the PIF's extensive investment in high-end luxury residential developments as prominent examples of how public investment pushes out private sector development. Moreover, their perception is that such developments do not have to adhere to the standard regulations and bureaucratic oversight. They accuse the PIF of illegally using labor and machinery owned by various ministries.

The intrusiveness of the Palestine Investment Fund into Palestinian society is extreme to the extent that the fund even refuses to relinquish control over a private primary school in Gaza. PIF representatives not only conduct commercial business through offices inside the school grounds but intrude to the level of changing student grades and affecting hiring and firing of teachers. (The black leather couches and expensive office equipment of the PIF stand in contrast to the stark, failing school desks in the adjacent room in the American International School in Gaza.) Another often-voiced allegation is that the PIF benefits from land appropriated from the ministries through Presidential decree, with no corresponding expenditure.

HAMAS & RECONCILIATION GOVERNMENT

The latest announcement represents the third attempt by Hamas and Fatah to reunite the West Bank and Gaza after the 2007 split. Significant disagreements remain and actual reconciliation of security forces and legal systems seems unlikely. Both sides, however, see critical upsides in reconciliation. The PLO seeks to reinforce its status as the representative of all of Palestine. Hamas desperately needs relief from its disastrous economic situation and its inability to meet payroll. In addition, the Hamas leadership feels that only a unity government will enhance its political isolation after the downfall of the like-minded Morsi presidency in Egypt and the decreasing support from a besieged Syria. Ironically, both the Hamas and the PLO are suffering from upward pressure from their respective Palestinian streets: Islamic Jihad and Salafists in Gaza, and the new generation of PLO activists in the West Bank, respectively.

U.S. law is clear regarding cutting off assistance should Hamas be participant in the government. Some observers, including in Israel believe that Palestinians might be able to buck the odds and form a government encompassing the West Bank and Gaza that clearly meets the Quartet's and American requirements, namely to clearly abdicate violence and recognize Israel. More likely, a new government would seek to fudge the issue by not having any upfront Hamas members.

It is in the interest of Palestinians and the United States for the Palestinian Authority to assert a single administration that effectively administers the West Bank and Gaza. However, the bar would need to be clearly set and the PA held accountable. Militias, such as the Hamas Izz ad-Din al-Qassam Brigades must be fully integrated into the national forces or disarmed. National elections should be held within six months. The election law should forbid participation by candidates who advocate violence.

While few give credence to recent threats by Abbas to abandon the PA following any cut off in U.S. assistance. The effect of a wholesale cut off would indeed be devastating. Decreasing international aid hurts the poor and marginalized sectors in a regressive manner. Local and international extremist groups would quickly move to exploit the situation. In addition to the question of the United States' diminished leverage, decreasing aid means decreasing our ability to support moderate elements and the new generation of Palestinians who will, at some point, be assuming control over their own destiny. Thus, instead of bluntly hammering the entire society, diplomatic, technical, and financial assistance can be used to foster a political and economic environment more receptive to reaching a durable peace with Israel.

IMPLICATIONS FOR POLICYMAKERS

Not to discount or ignore the impact of the occupation and Israeli policies, the Palestinian Authority squandered many opportunities to build a popular and effective administration that would help pave the way to peace. In addition, the U.S. and the donor community's overarching preoccupation with the negotiated peace process has, to some degree, enabled continuation of a dysfunctional public administration. Since the establishment of the PA, except for brief periods, the overarching goal of reaching a negotiated two-state solution has overshadowed efforts to promote a legitimate, effective participatory public administration that would serve as the foundation for an independent state and lead its constituency into a final peace agreement with Israel. Regardless of the prospects of a unity government or a reanimation of the peace process, "[T]he United States should move beyond short-term thinking – in which inconvenient Palestinian politics can and should be delayed because a negotiating breakthrough is just around the corner – that has afflicted its policies for decades." Rather, "[T]he United States should patiently support Palestinian Institution building and tolerate the political competition that must accompany it."

The Palestinian population is relatively young, educated and ambitious. This generation, which came of age during the second intifada, is largely progressive and comparatively independent. Like the rest of the region, they seek an enhancement of their quality of life, rule of law, equal opportunity, and the opportunity to participate in their own administration. To foster the conditions for peace, this generation needs to see the benefits of making peace with Israel.

Fostering political development within the PA does not mean accepting Hamas, in its current form, as a part of a unity government. The Palestinian Anti-Terrorism Act of 2006 and the principles espoused by the Quartet for recognition are clear: namely public acknowledgement of the state of Israel, adherence to past agreements, and renouncing violence. Any backtracking or weakening on these requirements would not only not be in the interest of the U.S., it would also be a disservice to the many Palestinians who continue to desire assistance in their ongoing fight against extremism.

As committee members are intimately aware, the United States is the leading provider of bilateral development assistance to the Palestinians, having committed over $5 billion since 1994. Within the international donor program, guided by the World Bank's "An Investment in Peace" paper in 2003, U.S. foreign assistance is part of the two-track approach to Middle East peace, which couples resumed political negotiations to establish a Palestinian state with support for the Palestinian state-building initiative through U.S. foreign assistance. USAID's efforts help to build a more democratic, stable, and secure region, benefiting Palestinians, Israelis, and Americans.

Despite its unintended consequence of propping up a presidential autocracy, this level of assistance, arguably the highest per capita of non-military aid, has succeeded in averting humanitarian catastrophes and mitigating environmental plagues. USG support for independent media fosters critical reporting. Education programs help foster anti-incitement as well as support underserved communities. In addition, USG – sponsored security assistance and training and police and prosecutorial programming plays a valuable role in countering extremists. Efforts promoting security cooperation between the Israelis and Palestinian security services continue to be critical to counter-terror efforts.

Continued external aid is needed to deal with the unique situation affecting the West Bank and Gaza, particularly the massive unemployment and lack of economic opportunity. However, the current pause in strategic negotiations may offer a time to reassess tactical activities and USG programming.

Although international trade facilitation and large economic projects offer high-profile activity and jobs, they tend to support the political and economic elite. Additional support for entrepreneurs and independent business, with a concentration on reaching underserved communities, may help to diversify the economy and be better received by local population. Devoting additional funding for rule of law programming may be useful to restore the confidence and feeling of general security in the general population.

In the weeks leading up to the 2006 parliamentary elections, USAID launched an effort to showcase the attributes of Fatah. This thinly veiled attempt to inform voters in a critical period did not have the desired effect. This time around, a more strategic approach to elections and campaigning may be warranted. The Palestinian body politic would definitely benefit from additional programming aimed at political party development, independent candidate training, and independent media.

There are also many tangible reform activities that could have positive impact as conditions in future assistance programs, such as:

1.   A participatory election law that precludes candidates that advocate violence.

2.   Audit of the civil service and pension payrolls.

3.   Disassociation of the Palestine Investment Fund from the President's office.

4.   Adding an office of a vice president.

5.   Allow PA ministers' free reign to appoint their own deputies and department heads without presidential interference.

The Palestinian Authority remains the best vehicle by which to bring a durable peace to the region. However, lacking a political mandate from its own constituency, the PA leadership will be unable and unwilling to make the difficult decisions needed to move from the status quo. Reform of the current public administration, combined with the backing of an active, prospering civil society will go a long way to support a diplomatic solution. To date, few Palestinians have benefitted from the two decades of the Oslo process. Enhancing the quality of life in the West Bank and Gaza should be the highest priority for the PA and international stakeholders.

Thank you again for this opportunity to offer some thoughts on the current situation in the Palestinian Authority. I would be happy to answer any questions you might have.

Mr. DeSantis. And the Chair now recognizes the gentleman from Florida, Mr. Wexler.

STATEMENT OF THE HONORABLE ROBERT WEXLER, PRESIDENT, S. DANIEL ABRAHAM CENTER FOR MIDDLE EAST PEACE (FORMER MEMBER OF CONGRESS)

Mr. Wexler. Thank you, Mr. Chairman, Ranking Member Schneider, members of the subcommittee. Thank you for the honor of allowing me to testify before a committee I truly cherish and in the company of several dear friends who I respect enormously.

Although 9 months have passed and negotiations between Israel and the Palestinians have stalled, what was true at the start of the talks is even truer today: Negotiations between Israel and the Palestinians remain in both sides' respective strategic interests.

For the Palestinians, there was and still is only one reality: The route to an independent state runs through a negotiated agreement with Israel. Neither seeking admission to international institutions nor threatening to dismantle the Palestinian Authority can achieve the dignity and justice Palestinians deserve in a state of their own.

For Israel, there was and still is only one reality: To secure its future as a Jewish and Democratic state, a viable independent and, yes, demilitarized Palestinian state must be realized.

So what do we do now? First, it is too soon to judge the nature of the reconciliation agreement between Fatah and Hamas. There, in fact, have been similar reconciliation agreements attempts in the past that were never implemented.

On Hamas, there is no debate. Hamas is a terrorist organization, no ifs, no ands, no buts. We need to appreciate, however, that the differences between Fatah and Hamas are as great as the differences between Israel and the Palestinians.

Israel's actual response to the reconciliation agreement is instructive. Prime Minister Netanyahu is no dove, but he has been careful to suspend the talks with the Palestinians and not cancel them outright.

And on Tuesday, Israel walked back from threats to impose sanctions on the Palestinian Authority. The Prime Minister knows that Israel is most secure when it is working in cooperation with Palestinian security forces.

Just this week, Palestinian forces uncovered and arrested four members of a terror cell in the West Bank that was plotting to attack Israelis.

Should Congress move now to defund the Palestinian Authority in response to the reconciliation agreement?

When I was in your shoes, I would have been quick to make a strong political statement condemning a new Palestinian Government that might include terrorists.

However, if Congress defunds the Palestinian Authority and the P.A. cannot pay its security forces and other bills, we hand a victory to Hamas.

A stated purpose of the reconciliation agreement is to conduct an election, a desperately needed election, in the Palestinian territories.

Should the Palestinians, in fact, return to the ballot box, we must bolster those Palestinians who renounce violence and recognize Israel's right to exist.

Cutting off U.S. funds now will depress the Palestinian economy, increase unemployment, and clearly advantage the objectives of the extremists. How does that help us? How does that help Israel?

We already have sufficient laws that prevent funding of terrorist organizations. Let those laws serve their purpose. This is not the time for hasty action.

In the immediate future, we should encourage the two sides to continue to deescalate the fraught situation and keep the window for a two-state solution open.

Moreover, all is not lost. Progress was, in fact, achieved on the core issues of borders and refugees during the recent negotiations.

Additionally, for the first time, the Arab League modernized the Arab Peace Initiative to accept the principle of land swaps, which would allow Israel to retain the major settlement blocs adjacent to the 1967 lines.

And after working with more than 150 experts at the Pentagon, General John Allen presented an extraordinary security package that, in a two-state outcome, would include measures to make Israel's eastern border as strong as any border in the world.

President Obama and Secretary Kerry deserve credit for initiating a credible process. It is now up to the two sides to build on what was achieved over the past year or that progress will slip away.

Pope John Paul said there were two possible solutions to the Arab-Israeli conflict, the realistic and the miraculous. The realistic would involve divine intervention. The miraculous, a voluntary agreement between the parties.

It is America's duty to keep pushing for the miraculous.

Thank you, Mr. Chairman.

Mr. DeSantis. Thank the gentleman.

[The prepared statement of Mr. Wexler follows:]

Testimony
The Honorable Robert Wexler
President, S. Daniel Abraham Center for Middle East Peace

House Foreign Affairs Committee
Subcommittee on the Middle East and North Africa

The Palestinian Authority, Israel and the Peace Process: What's Next

May 8, 2014

Chairman Ros-Lehtinen, Ranking Member Deutch, Members of the Subcommittee, thank you for the honor of testifying before a committee I truly cherish.

Although nine months have passed, and negotiations between Israel and the Palestinians have stalled, what was true at the start of the talks is even truer today: negotiations between Israel and the Palestinians remain in both sides' respective strategic interests.

For the Palestinians, there was and still is only one reality: the route to an independent state runs through a negotiated agreement with Israel. Neither seeking admission to international institutions, nor threatening to dismantle the Palestinian Authority can achieve the dignity and justice Palestinians deserve in a state of their own.

For Israel, there was and still is only one reality: to secure its future as a Jewish and democratic state, a viable, independent and demilitarized Palestinian state must be realized.

So what do we do now?

First, it is too soon to judge the nature of the reconciliation agreement between Fatah and Hamas. There have been similar reconciliation attempts in the past that were never implemented.

On Hamas, there is no debate: Hamas is a terrorist organization – no ifs, no ands, no buts. We need to appreciate, however, that the differences between Fatah and Hamas are as great as the differences between Israel and the Palestinians.

Israel's actual response to the reconciliation agreement is instructive. Prime Minister Netanyahu is no dove, but he has been careful to "suspend" the talks with the Palestinians, and not cancel them outright. And on Tuesday, Israel walked back from threats to impose sanctions on the Palestinian Authority.

The prime minster knows that Israel is most secure when it is working in cooperation with Palestinian security forces. Just this week, Palestinian forces uncovered and arrested four members of a terror cell in the West Bank that was plotting to attack Israelis.

Should Congress move now to defund the Palestinian Authority in response to the reconciliation agreement?

When I was in your shoes, I would have been quick to make a strong political statement condemning a new Palestinian government that might include terrorists.

However, if Congress defunds the PA, and the PA cannot pay its security forces and other bills, we hand a victory to Hamas.

A stated purpose of the reconciliation agreement is to conduct an election – a desperately needed election – in the Palestinian territories. Should the Palestinians return to the ballot box, we must bolster those Palestinians who renounce violence and recognize Israel's right to exist. Cutting off U.S. funds now will depress the economy and increase unemployment, clearly advancing the objectives of the extremists. How does that help us? How does that help Israel?

We already have sufficient laws that prevent the funding of terrorist organizations. Let those laws serve their purpose.

This is not the time for hasty action. In the immediate future, we should encourage the two sides to continue to deescalate the fraught situation, and keep the window for a two-state solution open.

Moreover, all is not lost. Progress was, in fact, achieved on the core issues of borders and refugees during the recent negotiations. Additionally, for the first time, the Arab League modernized the Arab Peace Initiative to accept the principle of land swaps, which would allow Israel to retain the major settlement blocs adjacent to the 1967 lines. And, after working with more than 150 experts at the Pentagon, General John Allen presented an extraordinary security plan that, in a two-state outcome, would include measures to make Israel's eastern border as strong as any border in the world.

President Obama and Secretary Kerry deserve credit for initiating a credible process. It is now up to the two sides to either build on what was achieved over the past year, or that progress will slip away.

Pope John Paul said there were two possible solutions to the Arab-Israeli conflict: the realistic and the miraculous. The realistic would involve divine intervention, the miraculous, a voluntary agreement between the parties. It is America's duty to keep pushing for the miraculous.

Mr. DeSantis. And we will begin the questioning.

We'll go to the gentleman from California. Mr. Rohrabacher is recognized for 5 minutes.

Mr. Rohrabacher. I like that, the miraculous. That is good.

All these things, like the progress that you mentioned, Bob, when the border swaps were approved, this is all just short term. They are meaningless unless there is this long-term recognition of the basic principle that is necessary to have peace.

And that is for the Palestinians to say, "Yes. Israel will exist." We are spending $400 million a year subsidizing the Palestinians over decades while they are being intransigent the whole time.

And, again, I am not sitting here rooting that the Palestinians come out losers in all of this. I think the winners are going to be Palestinians and Israelis living side by side and respecting each other's rights in a two-state solution.

But do you really think the United States—if there are only—if all we are seeing is short-term gains that don't mean anything unless you have that long-term understanding, we can't do that forever, can we?

Yes, Bob.

Mr. Wexler. I am not the spokesman of the Palestinian Authority. But, in 1988, the Palestinian Authority recognized Israel's right to exist. If they didn't, you wouldn't be voting to send money to the Palestinian Authority. That was a condition of American engagement with the Palestinian Authority.

So what we have here—I mean, your point, though, is well taken, I think, in a different respect. And that is: Should the Palestinians, in the context of the current negotiations, recognize Israel as a Jewish state, as a state in the context of mutuality of recognition? And the answer is absolutely "yes."

But we have to be fair, with all due respect. What is President Abbas's negotiation position on borders? His position is that he will and does recognize the State of Israel within the 1967 lines.

And, in fact, in the last round of negotiations under President Bush and—yet again, he offered a plan which gave Israel, of course, all of the 67 Israel plus roughly 2 percent of the West Bank.

So while you and I may not think that sufficiently incorporates enough of the settlement blocs into the State of Israel in terms of their internationally recognized borders, it is not fair to say that President Abbas has not recognized Israel's right to exist. He has.

The question is: Will he also deny, in effect, or give up the right of return? And that needs to be done in the context of a full agreement.

And, in fairness—in fairness to him, he had an interview not too long ago. President Abbas was born in Safed—in the Israeli holy city, the Jewish holy city, of Safed.

And he was asked, "Do you to expect to go back to Safed? And, if you do, under what terms?" And he said, "Yes. I hope to go back. But I know I'll go back as a tourist. I'm not going back to my home."

Now, the next day, there were all kinds of protests and the Palestinian Authority calling him a traitor.

Mr. ROHRABACHER. Right. And those people who were doing that were not in favor of peace with Israel.

The point is the right of return is a recognition of the right of Israel to exist. And until that right of return, that concept, "Well, yes. We will have an agreement and then we will have 3 million or 4 million more of our people come within those borders"—that is not a recognition of Israel.

And, again, I am hoping that someday you can have a Palestine and an Israel living side by side. And when they do say "a Jewish state of Israel," let's remember that all throughout the Middle East, you have got the Islamic state of so-and-so.

And that doesn't mean their rights of minorities aren't going to be protected in Israel. We all know that. When Israel says it is the Israeli—it is going to be a Jewish state, they are going to respect the rights of Muslims and respect the rights of Christians as well. We know that.

But, again, my time is—of questions, I've got 30 seconds left. Go to the other panelists.

Am I just off base in saying, until they say the right of return is gone, that they really have not recognized Israel?

Mr. SCHANZER. Look, I would just add this, Congressman Rohrabacher.

I think, actually, one of the biggest challenges we have right now is through the UNRWA program, the United Nations program that is designed to help Palestinian refugees.

What they have effectively done is they have perpetuated the refugee program. They have continued this so-called right of return challenge that we continue to face on the Palestinian side.

In other words, what you had after 1948 was a situation where there were 800,000 refugees. Today, thanks to the laws in place by UNRWA, there are more than 5 million.

Now, how is it that over the years these refugees have grown in number? This is an impossible number to assimilate. And so this is part of the problem that needs to be solved.

I should note that there is legislation that has been slowly winding its way through the Senate and, I think, also in the House, if I am not mistaken, that looks at redefining what a Palestinian refugee is.

It is no longer—it should no longer be okay to have the descendents of refugees, in other words, the children, the grandchildren, the great-grandchildren. That is how you get to 5 million. And those people should not have refugee status. They need to relinquish that.

And only the leadership of the Palestinian Authority, the PLO, can only—I think that that is the only message that can come from them, and that is how this is going to begin to change. Until then, you are going to have this tinderbox that you described.

Mr. DESANTIS. Gentleman's time has expired.

The Chair now recognizes the gentleman from Virginia, 5 minutes.

Mr. CONNOLLY. Thank you, Mr. Chairman. I am grateful for having today's hearing.

I want to welcome our colleague, Bob Wexler, back.

I share the concerns expressed by my colleagues as well as by supporters of both Israel and the Palestinian people.

Over the recent breakdown in the 9-month-old talks, which have been brokered by the United States, it is disappointing to see the dissolution—or seeming dissolution of this latest effort to achieve progress and a peaceful resolution of a long-standing conflict.

Achieving a two-state solution is in the best interests of both the Israeli and Palestinian peoples and it is central to U.S. efforts to restore stability in the region.

While there has been no shortage of finger-pointing, it appears the collective actions of both sides perhaps contributed to the erosion of any immediate chance to extend the talks further.

Some characterize the Palestinian Authority's resumption of activities to exceed the 15 multilateral treaties and conventions, which it had initially agreed to suspend in the midst of the peace talks, and then to announce a unity agreement with Hamas, designated as a terrorist organization by the United States, and, as Mr. Wexler said, no ifs, ands, or buts about it, and its refusal to recognize Israel's legitimacy clearly undermine the chance for real progress at least for now.

On the other side, some point to Israel's delay of the forced release of Palestinian prisoners, the final group of 104 who Israel agreed to release in exchange for Palestine suspending its international recognition efforts and Israel's continued settlement activities, as also undercutting the process.

Knowing how such actions from both sides would be negatively perceived by the other, I am going to be very curious as to the panel's views on whether the U.S. did all it could to manage the process.

And I have a full statement I put into the record. With unanimous consent, Mr. Chairman?

Mr. DeSANTIS. It will be so put in the record.

Mr. CONNOLLY. I thank you.

And I would like to give the opportunity to the panel on that last question.

Not for the purpose of finger-pointing or blame, but what could have, should have, the United States done differently or in addition or more of or less of that might have made a difference?

Dr. Schanzer.

Mr. SCHANZER. Thank you, Congressman Connolly.

I think that there is a lot of finger-pointing that is going on right now, and I think you are right to try to stay away from that.

I think it is instructive to look at the United States and its strategy and peacemaking. And I included this in my written remarks as well as my spoken remarks.

I think that the Iran issue casts a pall over the entire Middle East right now. It is the number one challenge. And I think that— but I should even note that it is not the only challenge. You have got a civil war in Syria. You have got a very unstable Egypt. You have got Arab Spring issues.

There are only so many issues that we can solve. And I say that as the United States appears to be retreating from the Middle East, not looking to engage even more. And so how we decided that we would be able to take on all of these issues and do them successfully is still very unclear to me.

My approach would have been to be somewhat more modest with the objectives, to have a quiet approach to diplomacy, not to set a 9-month window with an expiration date at the end, you know, first proclaiming that you are going to end the conflict, well, then, you know, have to downgrade and start to talk about having a framework agreement.

I think it was all ill-advised. I think we bit off more than we could chew. I think that, if we do get back into the business of peacemaking, I think it needs to be done more quietly. And I suspect, by the way, it is happening right now anyway.

And, in the process, as Mr. Prince and I both discussed in our testimonies, there needs to be a focus on the change in leadership inside the Palestinian Authority for a more legitimate government.

Mr. CONNOLLY. I couldn't agree with you more, everything you said.

Congressman Wexler, did you want to comment?

Mr. WEXLER. Yes, please.

First, I will agree, there is no reason to go back and assign blame. One of the things that I think Secretary Kerry, though, did right was that he effectively kept the talks secret for a great period of time, and I think that assisted both sides.

But there is a misnomer here that needs to be recognized. Secretary Kerry, President Obama didn't drag anybody to a peace table. The Israelis and the Palestinians both wanted to be there from the beginning. For separate reasons, it was in their interests. And then we became, obviously, the facilitator.

But let me take up on a point that the two gentlemen raised, and that is a change of Palestinian leadership. Well, in order to have a change that I think all of us would be comfortable with, you need to have a democratic process, and we need to be pragmatic about how a democratic process comes about in the context of the Palestinian Authority or the Palestinian territories.

In order to hold it in the West Bank, you need Fatah to agree. In order to hold it in Gaza, you need Hamas to agree. In order to hold it in East Jerusalem, you need the Israelis to agree.

Well, how are you going to get Fatah and Hamas to agree to an election unless you have a reconciliation, understanding of some sort?

So we just need to be honest amongst ourselves. If we are going to demand a change in leadership—and we certainly want that leadership change to be democratic—then we need to understand there needs to be some accommodation with groups that we label as a terrorist. Otherwise, you are not going to have an election.

So we at least need to be honest with ourselves. And the Israelis have to agree to have it in East Jerusalem, along with the two Palestinian sides.

Mr. CONNOLLY. Thank you so much.

And, Mr. Chairman, I wonder if you would just indulge Mr. Prince an opportunity to respond. My questioning is over. And I thank both the chairman and my friend——

Mr. DESANTIS. Gentleman will have 1 minute to respond.

Mr. CONNOLLY. I thank the chair.

Mr. PRINCE. Thank you, Congressman Connolly.

I would agree with both the previous comments. One, there needs to be a democratic process, there needs to be elections. And, two, I think we did bite off more than we can chew in the recent go-around.

The basic points of a departure in a deal is that both sides feel a benefit and really want to reach the end of a deal. I would argue that President Abbas, from the start of 9 months ago, was not—was more interested in the process than he was a final status agreement.

I do believe there were modest steps that could have been taken, could have been agreed upon, that would have pushed both sides together, but President Abbas did not believe from the very beginning that he had the right or ability to reach a final status agreement. And, therefore, the gamesmanship—not to mention the Israeli side—the gamesmanship continued on.

There needs to be, as Congressman Wexler mentioned, some sort of democratic process to restore some sort of unity, cohesion within the Palestinian community. Right now, it is dysfunctional.

And I don't believe any Palestinian leader that would emerge from the Fatah leadership will be brave enough, either from a security standpoint or a political standpoint, to reach a final status agreement.

Mr. DESANTIS. Thank the gentleman. Time has expired.

The Chair will recognize himself for 5 minutes.

You know, in terms of this recognizing Israel, I mean, it is crucial. Yes. I acknowledge they are willing to recognize some geographic entity called Israel.

But if you don't recognize Israel's right to exist as a Jewish state, then we are not in a situation where you are going to have a long-term peaceful resolution.

I mean, the whole purpose of Israel being a refuge is that it would be a Jewish state. And they have consistently refused to recognize that.

And I will give some of the witnesses a chance. I don't know if that represents the broad view of the Palestinian Arabs in the area.

I certainly believe that most people in Gaza do not believe Israel has a right to exist as a Jewish state. But that has been the biggest roadblock.

There have been opportunities to have an Arab state throughout history. It seems like the desire to not have a Jewish state always trumped the desire to have a Palestinian state, and I don't see evidence that we have gotten beyond that.

So let me ask you, Congressman Wexler. You talked about you would not move to defund it because, you know, you acknowledge Hamas as a terrorist group, but you are just not sure how this is going to shake out. It is true in the past there have been kind of attempts at unity that have fizzled.

So at what point would you be willing to pull the trigger and say that we shouldn't be rewarding this type of behavior with Hamas?

Mr. WEXLER. If Hamas, in fact, joins a unity government and Hamas has not in the context of that government accepted the three principles adopted by the Quartet—recognize Israel's right to

exist, renounce violence, and incorporate all of the aggrieved under-
standings between the sides—then the law is clear. There will not
be funding.

But at this point——

Mr. DeSantis. But that recognition—you would not require that
to be recognizing Israel as a Jewish state, just recognizing——

Mr. Wexler. No. There is no requirement to recognize Israel as
a Jewish state in any type of understanding that has previously existed between the Israelis and the Palestinians.

We need to be, again, honest amongst ourselves. When you say
"recognize Israel as a Jewish state," do I recognize Israel as a Jewish state? Of course, I do. It is the Jewish state. Israel is the Jewish state.

But where is that state? What makes it a Jewish state? It is a
Jewish state because it is a majority made up of Jewish residents.

Well, is that state the 1967 lines incorporating the settlement
blocs, incorporating the settlements, or is it the 67 lines plus the
West Bank and Gaza?

So we need to be honest. When you talk about recognizing Israel
as a Jewish state, which I am all in favor of—don't get me wrong—
it is not so simple on the other side.

And I think we ought to take a look at the language of the Arab
Peace Initiative, which is quite forthcoming. While it doesn't say
Israel is a Jewish state and it doesn't talk directly about the right
of return, what it says is the right of return will have an agreed-
upon resolution.

Every Arab country in the world has put that forward. When
they say "agreed-upon resolution," that means Israel must agree.
Well, they know Israel will never agree to take back 5 million refugees or even 800,000 refugees. So there has been movement.

Mr. DeSantis. And let me go to Dr. Schanzer.

What is your view? I mean, do you think, one, that moving to
defund the aid, if this unity movement continues? And do you think
people in Congress should be conditioning tax dollars?

I mean, should we demand that there be a recognition that Israel
has a right to exist as a Jewish state, given that that seems to be
a precondition certainly for Prime Minister Netanyahu and I know
many of us in this body.

Mr. Schanzer. Mr. Chairman, thank you.

Look, I would say that the difference between a Jewish state and
just a state that deserves to exist—in my mind, there is really no
difference.

And my problem has always been with the Palestinian Nationalist movement, that it has been more based on destruction of the
State of Israel than the creation of something, i.e., a Palestinian
state.

We know more about what they don't like and how angry they
are than about what it is that they want to create. And so that has
been my approach to this problem all along.

Would it help if the Palestinians acknowledged that and put the
Israelis' minds at ease? Absolutely. Should it be one of our pre-
conditions? Look, I will leave that to you.

But let me just answer to one thing that Congressman Wexler said. The idea of acknowledging a technocratic government that includes figures approved by Hamas is a slippery slope.

The idea that you could allow the technocratic government to take place just because you want to see elections happen, that is basically acknowledging Hamas and it is opening the door to allow Hamas to come in as a legitimate player in the next elections, which is something that we have to avoid at all costs.

Mr. PRINCE. I would definitely agree that the distinction between recognition of a Jewish state and recognizing the existence and the independence of the State of Israel is very nuanced and something that I think shouldn't preclude the United States from enforcing the law right now.

Privately, Palestinians do—and including in Gaza, they do talk of the right of return. As Congressman Wexler says, it is sort of pie in the sky to say that Israel is going to accept millions of refugees. And they also talk about Israel as a Jewish state in Gaza City as well as Ramallah.

What they don't say so is publicly. The leadership—and the Palestinian papers released a few years ago by Al Jazeera also reinforced this concept.

We are talking about the Palestinian community as a unified group, and that doesn't exist today. The right of return and recognizing Israel, I would argue, is a non-issue privately. No Palestinian leadership worth its salt on any side really says that those issues still exist today.

Mr. DeSANTIS. I thank the gentleman. My time is expired. So I thank you for that.

And the Chair will now recognize the gentleman from Illinois, Mr. Schneider, 5 minutes.

Mr. SCHNEIDER. Thank you, Mr. Chair.

Again, thank you to the witnesses for being here.

Congressman Wexler, with all due respect, I think Israel was created as a Jewish state. We celebrated the 66th anniversary of its creation this past Monday.

It had its foundation on November 29th, 1947, in U.N. Resolution 181, a Jewish state and an Arab state. The Jews accepted that. The Arabs did not. And that is the battle that is being fought today.

So I think the question really is: When will the Palestinians not recognize, but accept, that Israel is a Jewish state and accept that the right of return is a non-starter, as was discussed?

I think it is also important to emphasize that, as you said, Dr. Schanzer, any P.A. reconciliation between Fatah and Hamas that includes a Hamas, that doesn't recognize the Quartet conditions, the three conditions as you noted, is unacceptable and cannot continue to have U.S. support.

But the purpose of this meeting is really about what is next. It was in the title. And I would like to focus on what is next.

A year ago—exactly a year ago Salaam Fayyad stepped down as Prime Minister. For many years, I think the conversations in this committee, around the country, were that the future prospects for a Palestinian state depended on the aspirations of Fayyad of building the institutions. He is no longer there. He was forced out.

Hamdallah was put in replacement for Fayyad. We don't hear about him at all.

What does the future of a Palestinian Authority, Palestinian Government, look like without people committed to building the institutions? And who might there be that would build those institutions? Dr. Schanzer?

Mr. SCHANZER. Thank you, Congressman Schneider.

I would just concur that we have a real problem, that the exit of the Fayyad—look it, in many ways, this was the deflation of the Palestinian Nationalist project, at least one that had a direction and a vision.

The defeat of Fayyad was a victory for the corruption and the ossified approach to government that Mr. Abbas has embraced over these years.

Rami Hamdallah, the new Prime Minister, is a neophyte and really does not serve in that role of checks and balances against the presidency, which was always the intended role of the Prime Minister, was to check that absolute power over the Palestinian presidency.

And on top of that, what we have is a very troubling development where the new Deputy Prime Minister, Mohammed Mustafa, who also happens to be the head of the PIF, has become a very powerful guy. You see this centralization of power again, and that is the concern.

The other concern is that there is just no political space for new parties, new figures, to emerge. And so you have this monopoly over power without even allowing for new voices to come onto the scene, to debate, to get into that clash of ideas that is so necessary for democratic reform.

And so we have got a real problem on our hands, and I have to say that American policy has reinforced this, that we continue to look at Mr. Abbas as the only one who can deliver and, therefore, continue to give him whatever he needs. And so it has compounded these problems over time.

When Abbas goes, there is no plan for what happens next. There is no leadership. There is no succession. It is going to be a vacuum, and it will be on our heads for failing to have planned for that moment.

Mr. SCHNEIDER. Mr. Prince, I will turn to you, but let me just interject.

Dr. Schanzer talked about Mr. Mustafa rising, and I think that was somewhat predictable. Mustafa was the first choice, but I think, because of his engagement with PIF, he was not palatable, if you will. So Hamdallah kind of fills the titular role, but Mustafa has the power.

Now we are looking forward. Abbas is 79 years old. There needs to be some commitment from the Israelis to move toward peace. They are going to have a partner on the other side who will be there for a long term. What are the prospects?

And, Mr. Prince, Congressman Wexler, I would like both of your comments.

Mr. PRINCE. Well, first of all, as members of the committee noted, there is a significant constituency that remains for peace in both West Bank and Gaza.

50

The problem is they are not currently represented. With Abbas leaving office prior to the next election, there will be a significant vacuum. There will be infighting and there will be debate between the older generation and the newer generation.

The question is whether the newer generation, as Dr. Schanzer mentioned, has the political space to actually represent themselves and be part of the process.

I believe that that is something that we should start preparing for now. If we don't, there will be a resumption of not only infighting, but probably some of the violence that happened in 2007 in Gaza will definitely go to the West Bank.

There is not going to be an L—PLO, Tunisian—they call them the Abus—that are going to run the Palestinian Authority in the next time around. To be a partner for peace, we need to look to this peace constituency and the vast population.

Mr. SCHNEIDER. If I may give Congressman Wexler a minute.

Mr. DESANTIS. Yep.

Mr. WEXLER. Very quickly, another aspect of what Secretary Kerry, of course, was attempting to do is, while economics are not a replacement for political achievements, a very important part of his diplomatic initiative was attracting investment to the West Bank.

And, in fact, extraordinary commitments were made mostly by American but, also, by some European companies to engage in the West Bank.

If you go to Ramallah today, if you go to Jenin today, if you go to other population centers today in the West Bank, they are by and large far more law abiding, peaceful, and successful than they were, say, 10 years ago.

What I think needs to happen in the future—Israel, thankfully, has had some extraordinary energy finds. Those energy finds, particularly in certain areas, ought to be talked about in terms of sharing with the Palestinians.

You are going to need to build a port, an air facility to allow transport in and out of an emerging Palestinian economy.

But these things are very difficult to do when the Palestinians don't have their own government in effect to exercise the authority to do it.

And if I may just respond to Mr. Schneider, respectfully, I would be careful when referring to the U.N. Partition Plan in support of Israel as a Jewish state.

Again, you consider Israel a Jewish state. I consider Israel a Jewish state. But the Jewish state of Israel that was created in the United National Partition Plan in terms of the boundaries is not a boundaries plan that Israel would accept today, and you wouldn't and I wouldn't.

So we have to be careful in terms of—I would respectfully suggest, when we are talking about what is a Jewish state, it is not so simple.

Mr. SCHNEIDER. I appreciate that.

But when David Ben Gurion declared independence on May 14, he declared the Jewish state of Israel.

Mr. WEXLER. Yes.

Mr. SCHNEIDER. It has stayed that. It will remain that. And any negotiated peace between the Palestinians must assure that.

Mr. WEXLER. I agree.

Mr. SCHNEIDER. Thank you very much.

Mr. DESANTIS. The gentleman's time is expired.

The Chair now recognizes the gentleman from North Carolina, Mr. Meadows, for 5 minutes.

Mr. MEADOWS. Thank you, Mr. Chairman.

Thank each of you for your testimony.

Mr. Schanzer, I want to go to you. I saw, I guess, reaction to Mr. Wexler's response just in your face. So I will give you a few minutes to respond.

Mr. SCHANZER. Sure. Thank you, Congressman Meadows.

Look it, I would just say this to Congressman Wexler. The idea of ensuring continued financial assistance or financial incentives to the Palestinian Authority right now is putting the cart before the horse.

Without the reform that is necessary, the $4 billion that the United States promised the Palestinians, should an agreement be struck, would have been wasted.

In many ways, this was actually a helpful step by not allowing the peace process to go through before the reform process could take place. It would have been a sinkhole.

We have seen what has happened before where hundreds of millions, in fact, billions, of dollars have been plowed into the Palestinian Authority over the last 20 years.

Since 1994, we have provided billions of dollars. The Europeans have provided billions of dollars. The Arab Gulf States have provided billions of dollars.

And we do not see a Palestinian Authority that is in much better shape today to perform the tasks of governance in a way that they would be respected in the Palestinian Authority or internationally.

And so, again, this underscores the same problem that I have been focusing on here at this subcommittee, at the committee level as well, that there is a huge problem of legitimacy, a huge problem of corruption, inside the Palestinian Authority that must be tackled if we are going to be able to move forward.

Mr. MEADOWS. All right. Let me go a little bit further, because I just returned from the region and three things concern me greatly

.

One, we continue to spend money. And it is a complex situation. Everybody knows that. If it was easy, it would have been solved long ago.

However, I went into a terror tunnel that had just been constructed with moneys that we probably sent to folks in Gaza. A mile and a half long, concrete floors, concrete walls, concrete ceilings, communication, rail, lights.

And, yet, here we are talking about economic development and, yet, this mile-and-a-half-long tunnel, probably built with American taxpayers' moneys, with the sole purpose of coming up in the middle of a field so they could abduct Jewish settlers at a—not settlers—Jewish folks in a kibbutz troubled me.

At what point do we say enough is enough?

Mr. SCHANZER. Well, Congressman Meadows, I would just add this. The money has been cut off largely to the Palestinian territory of Gaza. We have done a pretty good job of bottling that up.

There are some things—and, actually, Mr. Prince can speak to this—where there is money that has been going through to the power plant inside the Gaza Strip that is coming from the Palestinian Authority, which, of course, we fund.

Mr. MEADOWS. Right.

Mr. SCHANZER. And so there are some millions of dollars that are still leaking through. There is also the pressure that is placed on the Israelis to ensure that the cement and other goods get through to the Gaza Strip and, if it doesn't, then, of course, the Israelis get blamed for humanitarian——

Mr. MEADOWS. But therein is the thing. It is meant that we are getting there and it is being built in tunnels to come back at the very people who are providing it.

Mr. SCHANZER. That is right. That is right.

But I would actually just add one more thought, and that is that the top sponsors of Hamas right now are two U.S. allies. And this needs to be addressed.

You have Qatar and Turkey. They are now the two top sponsors and financiers of the Hamas organization. These are not allies any longer if this is what they are doing, and we have yet to address that. I think it is a serious problem.

Mr. MEADOWS. So, Mr. Prince, you would agree we need to address that in terms of Qatar and Turkey?

Mr. PRINCE. I agree. I think Qatar is one of the most pressing issues today. I happened to be in Gaza when the Royal Family visited some time ago.

With the change in relationship with the Egyptian Government, Qatar remains—to a lesser extent, the Iranian money—Qatar remains the largest financier of society in Gaza.

I would—just to go back to the question of tunnels and economic developments—or assistance, cutting off U.S. assistance leads people to increased dependency. We have the humanitarian issue, and we end up spending money in many different ways indirectly.

The question of the large economic development program proposed by Secretary Kerry, I don't believe, as Dr. Schanzer said, would have a positive impact on Palestinian society.

From an economic development standpoint, I spent years going through almost every commercial enterprise in West Bank and Gaza. The region can't absorb that amount of money.

Large infrastructure projects, like Congressman Wexler mentioned, look nice. They help the leadership. But they are not filtering down to providing durable jobs to local Palestinians.

And until we focus on that, we are not going to solve the problem. So the question of assistance is not cutting it off, but doing it smarter.

Mr. MEADOWS. Okay. And my time is expired.

So I would ask for the record if you would respond in writing in terms of what can we do about the incitement that is going on each and every day within that group. Because it is hard to get a negotiated deal when you are adding fuel to the fire, so to speak.

I will yield back, Mr. Chairman. Thank you.

Mr. DeSantis. The gentleman's time is expired.

The Chair now recognizes the gentleman from California, Mr. Vargas, for 5 minutes.

Mr. Vargas. Thank you very much, Mr. Chairman. Thank you for the opportunity to speak.

I want to thank the witnesses.

And, in particular, I want to thank Congressman Wexler. Thank you for being here. And, in particular, I would like to thank you for the quote of Pope Francis.

I am a former Jesuit myself in an ocean that the realistic is the divine intervention. I like that. It is probably true. The miraculous would be the voluntary agreement.

And you have been somewhat of a stickler here for details; so, I am going to be a little bit of a stickler with you, if you don't mind.

You have been using the date 1967 and 67 interchangeably. It is not. Israel is one of the few nations where both of those dates make sense. You can talk about the Israel of 1967, and you can talk about the Israel of 67. The Israel of 67 is much, much, much larger. Remember, it was a country in 67. So you do have to be careful when you use it.

I hear the President and others talking about the 67 lines. Well, the 67 lines would really tick off the neighbors because that would be a very, very large Israel today, the Northern Kingdom and the Southern Kingdom.

But, anyway, all of that aside, I do want to talk about this within the context of Iran because, you know, to me, it almost seems trite that we are arguing about this.

The reality is that Israel can take care of itself and, interestingly, Israel can also secure the Palestinians. One of the things that people don't talk about, but—you know, a lot of the Palestinians have it pretty darn good because Israel supports them.

You don't think that they would need to be protected from their neighbors, just ask Syrians, you know, "How do you do out there by yourself?" You know, it is a pretty mean neighborhood.

So we are trying to get to a peace. And you say it is in the interest of both, but it almost seems trite within the context of this existential threat that Iran poses to Israel and, ultimately, the threat it poses to ourselves.

Would you comment on that, Congressman, in particular.

Mr. Wexler. The threat of a nuclear-armed Iran is in and of itself, in my humble estimation, the most important endeavor that we must seek to defang, to defeat.

And while, yes, in any sense of reality, an Israeli Prime Minister, as would an American President, in the context of a region must consider all of these facts.

But we have been very careful—when I say "we," I think most of us on the American side that hold Israel's security very dear—we have been very careful never to mix the two.

The fact of the matter is the Israeli-Palestinian conflict, the resolution of that conflict is in the interest of both the Israelis and the Palestinians and on the merits of the conflict itself.

Because if we have learned anything from the Arab Spring, it should be that the Israeli-Palestinian conflict is not the cause of all of the root of evil in the region. It is one distinct set of circumstances that respectfully should be handled on its own based on its own merits.

Now, in reality, an Israeli Prime Minister certainly will consider the range of options in terms of what progress or non-progress is made with Iran. Clearly, that is the case.

And, unfortunately, it seems we were unable to make great progress on the Israel-Palestinian front prior to the culmination or the non-culmination of the talks with Iran.

But I think it would be a mistake if we joined the two together, the Israeli-Palestinian conflict and the Iranian nuclear program, in a way in which both had to be dealt with in some type of simultaneous or comparable way. I don't think that would benefit either the Israelis or the Palestinians.

Mr. VARGAS. Dr. Schanzer?

Mr. SCHANZER. Thank you.

I would just respond in this way, that the United States has had the ability to impose its will on the Israelis and Palestinians only at times when it has been able to demonstrate strength.

I think about the aftermath of the 1991 Gulf War and how, at that point, the United States looked invincible. And it was at that point also that the Arab states, the Palestinians and Israelis, got in line and began to work through this—what is now known as the Oslo Process.

We have a problem now that we look weaker than we have in recent memory. We do not appear to be able to have our way, which, really, when you think about the Iraq war, you think about Afghanistan, the war on terror, we have not enforced our own red lines in Syria. We can't seem to be able to solve this Iranian problem. We have a credibility problem right now. We need some wins.

My sincere belief is that, if we begin to take care of some of these problems—look it, whether it is the Iran problem, whether it is the Syria problem, whether it is bringing some order back to the Arab world after the Arab Spring, whatever it is, if we begin to do that, I believe it will become that much easier to start to get the Palestinians and Israelis to take this peace process seriously.

Mr. VARGAS. Thank you.

Mr. Prince, I apologize. My time has expired, but I was going to go to you.

Thank you, Mr. Chairman.

Mr. DESANTIS. The gentleman's time is expired.

The Chair now recognizes the gentleman from Florida, Mr. Yoho, for 5 minutes.

Mr. YOHO. Thank you, Mr. Chairman.

Gentlemen, I appreciate you being here.

Let me start with the money that we have invested in the Palestinian Authority since 1988, roughly $5 billion. Last year approximately $500 million was given to the Palestinian Authority in the name of peace, is what I like to think, you know.

The people back home don't want us sending any money overseas, especially in this economic crisis that we are having here.

Yet, in this room, a couple—about a month ago, in this very room, sitting right where you guys are, there was a gentleman talking about Resolution 21 and 23 in the Palestinian Authority loosely knit government laws that pays criminals that have created crimes of terrorism against Americans and Israeli citizens that are sitting in Israeli prisons.

The larger the act of terrorism, the larger the stipend they get. I think the average was $3,600. I have heard rumors of up to $10,000 a month when the average income in that area is around $5,000.

So we put in a resolution that says all funding to the Palestinian Authority gets cut until they remove Resolution 21 and 23.

Starting with you, Dr. Schanzer, I would like to hear your thoughts, and Mr. Prince, and Congressman Wexler. What effect would that have?

Mr. SCHANZER. The cutting of funding?

Mr. YOHO. To stop it.

If we are giving this money in the name of peace and they are promoting terrorism—you know, if you steal a loaf of bread, you go to prison. But if you commit a crime of terrorism and kill somebody, you go to prison and get a check.

And I think that is just reprehensible, that the American taxpayers are flipping the bill. And I know it goes into a fungible pot and they say, ''We are not using your money.'' I don't buy it. If you want our money, you need to stop promoting that kind of activity.

Mr. SCHANZER. Congressman Yoho, you are absolutely correct. Here is the problem. And, I mean, there are a couple of problems here.

Number one, what Mr. Abbas has done is he has actually delivered on peace. In other words, he brought an end to the Intifada in 2005. From 2000 to 2005, there was violence raging everywhere, and he was the leader.

After Yasser Arafat died, he was able to bring all of those different militias under the control of the Palestinian Authority. He, you know, made sure to disarm them.

And so, in that sense, the Israelis are much happier with his leadership and—as are we, I think, you know, generally speaking.

The problem is that, even though he has brought an end to the violence, he has maintained a culture of violence, nevertheless. And so that means paying off the terrorists who are in jail. It means the incitement that we see in mosque sermons and on television.

And so there is a baseline of hatred that Mahmoud Abbas has maintained and we have, to a certain extent, underwritten this. The problem now moving forward is what do you do about it.

You know, if we zero out Palestinian funding, then here is the big problem. You are going to have someone else come in and they are going to be worse.

More than likely, you are going to see the Saudis, the Iranians, the Qataris, the Turks. They are all going to come in and they are not even going to hold the Palestinians to account at all.

The important thing from my perspective, if we are going to keep the funding going, we need to make sure that we have tighter controls. We need to demand performance. And, in my opinion, we have just simply failed to do so.

Mr. YOHO. Mr. Prince.

Mr. PRINCE. I would definitely agree. The issue of prisoners is extremely dicey. Mahmoud Abbas has basically guaranteed security

56

through the old-time-mafia type of way of delivering brown bags of cash to people, and that includes families of political prisoners.

Mr. YOHO. Right. We have read about those.

Mr. PRINCE. And that has continued today. At least Arafat demanded something in return. Mahmoud Abbas, usually it is just to support acquiescence to his leadership.

The wholesale cutoff, as Dr. Schanzer said, presents a wide variety of problems. It is diminished leverage. It leaves a void.

The degree of dependency right now on international assistance doesn't really allow for a wholesale cutoff because aid agencies or extremists groups will come in to serve them.

I would argue, though, that there are a significant amount of conditions we should be putting on aid so that it is not fungible.

Mr. YOHO. I agree. I think get rid of Resolution 21 and 23 and we will get along fine. But until you stop promoting terrorism, I don't see how you are going to get peace.

And, you know, you had touched on something else—and I think you are right on—is we see a weakened America and we see an emboldened other part of the world, and they are stepping up.

And what effect do you think the Iran negotiations over the nuclear weapons and—right where we are at right now—what effect does that have on the security of the Israel and Palestinian area?

Go ahead, Congressman Wexler. You haven't had a chance.

Mr. DESANTIS. The gentleman's time is expired.

Mr. YOHO. I am sorry. My time is expired.

Mr. DESANTIS. Go ahead and take 30 seconds.

Mr. WEXLER. Well, first, I would agree that no American taxpayer's money should be going to fund terrorist families directly or indirectly, and any way in which you can go about to prevent that is an admirable attempt.

But I would also respectfully suggest you vote for this—I don't want to mischaracterize you. You say you vote for this because you are about achieving peace.

Well, I would suggest it really should be more than just peace at this point. It should be peace and, when not peace, at least security.

And we need to be realistic that there are forces within the Palestinian society that, in fact, support violence in a very overt way and there are those that oppose it in an overt way.

And those that oppose it are not necessarily Boy Scouts and they are not necessarily people you and I would vote for, but they oppose violence. And that is what President Abbas has done.

And so, when given the choice of the two teams that unfortunately we have at this point, if there becomes a third team or a fourth, then let's go for it.

But now we have got the Hamas team, and there is nothing good about that team. And then you got the Fatah team, which has all kinds of warts and all sorts of problems, but they oppose violence.

Mr. DESANTIS. The gentleman's time is expired.

The Chair now recognizes the gentlewoman from New York, Ms. Meng, for 5 minutes.

Ms. MENG. Thank you to our speakers for being here and to Congressman Wexler. It is an honor to hear from all of you.

While we are on the topic of aid, I am just curious. How much—are the Palestinian people aware of the aid that the United States gives them and how much do we give them?

Mr. SCHANZER. Congresswoman Meng, they are very aware. And they are also very aware of how little of it trickles down to them, and that is ultimately, I think, one of the greatest challenges that we face.

So here you have a Palestinian leadership that has brought in this $5 billion that we have heard about throughout the afternoon.

There has been a significant investment on the part of the Europeans, Arab states, et cetera, and it has been a sinkhole.

The middle class has not found a way to benefit from it. The lower class has been kept in refugee camps and in squalor.

And so the problem is creating a system whereby these funds can actually find their way to the right people. And under this leadership—and Congressman Wexler mentioned that the Fatah faction has warts. That is an understatement.

In other words, as long as the Fatah faction holds sway, they are going to withhold these funds. They are going to prevent these funds from reaching the middle and lower classes.

And that, in turn, perpetuates conflict. That is something that needs to stop. And, again, that is all about leadership. It is about preparing for that next generation of Palestinian leaders.

We should be making sure that they have the oxygen, the ability now, to present their ideas, and that is something that we have failed to deliver on for the Palestinian people.

And it is for that reason that, despite the billions of dollars that we have provided to the Palestinians, they still resent us. They think that we are on the side of Abbas.

Mr. PRINCE. If I may, Congresswoman Meng, I agree wholeheartedly. Every Palestinian is aware of the assistance provided by the United States, whether it is direct, indirect, through the United Nations or any other agency.

The question of whether it is viewed positively—and that is something that you can trace back from the inception of the P.A., that the general population has viewed these assistance programs less and less positively since the time of Arafat.

If you go back to the 2006 elections in which Hamas emerged victoriously, there was a USAID program to announce new projects very close—during the campaign period close to the elections.

It was a relatively thinly veiled attempt to inform the voters of the value of the assistance and the relationship with the United States. You could track the polls when those programs were announced, the decrease in support for Mahmoud Abbas and old-time Fatah.

The belief is that our assistance programs on security, environmental and health are central, critical, useful. Our assistance on democracy and governance and economic development has largely been siphoned off or used to support the powers that be and have not filtered down to the local population.

Mr. WEXLER. If I may?

Mr. DeSANTIS. Sure.

Mr. WEXLER. Secretary Kerry's approach, the diplomatic effort that he just led, was a multifaceted approach. He took on the political issues, he took on the diplomatic-related political issues, he took on the economic issues, and he took on civil society often in partnership with our European allies.

And under ideal circumstances, you address every aspect of Palestinian Authority simultaneously to build the kind of society that we have been talking about. The problem is, at least for the time being, that has broken down.

So the question is: How can you salvage as much positive results as humanly possible? And the reality is, unfortunately, that Hamas plays a role within Gaza that is completely unacceptable to us, to the Europeans and, of course, to the Israelis and, in many respects, unacceptable to President Abbas himself.

So the question is: How do we devise a strategy where we get to the point—the type of accountability that these gentlemen rightfully are highlighting? And, unfortunately, it is very difficult to do in a non-democratic atmosphere.

Ms. MENG. Thank you.

What steps has President Abbas taken over the past 9 months to prepare the Palestinian people for peace? And is there—how much support is there amongst these people for a peace deal?

Mr. DESANTIS. The gentlewoman's time is expired.

I know we just called the vote. So I am going to recognize——

Ms. MENG. We are not coming back?

Mr. DESANTIS. No. No. No. We are going to continue. But I want to make sure. I don't think that we will reconvene after the votes.

So I will recognize the gentleman from Arkansas, Mr. Cotton, for 5 minutes.

Mr. COTTON. Thank you. Dr. Schanzer, I noticed that you were shaking your head in apparent disagreement with Mr. Wexler's comments on Secretary Kerry's actions.

Do you care to elaborate on your head-shaking?

Mr. SCHANZER. Apparently, I have been somewhat expressive this afternoon.

Thank you, Congressman Cotton.

Look it, this is where I would disagree. I don't believe that Secretary Kerry's approach was multifaceted. I think that Secretary Kerry, while I believe that he was absolutely earnest in his attempts at peacemaking, fell into a familiar trap.

I recently wrote a book where I went around and I interviewed former peacemakers, from Dennis Ross, to Aaron David Miller, to Elliott Abrams, and they all basically said the same thing. And I believe we saw a reprise of that with Secretary Kerry, and that is the emphasis of the transaction over the transformation.

What do I mean by that? We continue to aim for that handshake on the White House lawn. Right? You think about these grand— you know, maybe winning that Nobel Prize, redrawing the map. And in the process, you don't get down to that less-than-sexy approach of state-building on the Palestinian side.

We continue to ignore the fact that these are basically autocrats, that these are kleptocrats. And, look it, if you really think that this was a multifaceted approach, ask yourself: Why was it that we didn't talk about preparing for new elections? Why was it that we didn't talk about preparing for the exit of Mahmoud Abbas, who is now so many years past the end of his term?

I mean, we pinned our hopes on one guy who had already passed his expiration date. That is not about reform. It is not about state-building.

And so we ignored the transformation again in order to get that transaction done. We need to learn how to walk and chew gum, and I don't believe that this administration did that this time around.

Mr. WEXLER. If I may.

Mr. COTTON. Yes, you may.

Mr. WEXLER. Secretary Kerry didn't talk about a full-fledged election because, in order to have a full-fledged election in the Palestinian territories, you need to have Hamas's agreement and we don't deal, rightfully so, with Hamas.

Now, we could redo—or attempt to try to redo what was done. And I do not say this in a critical fashion toward President Bush.

But President Abbas came to President Bush the first time around and said, "Should I include Hamas in the election?" And President Bush, for all the right reasons—I am not criticizing—said, "Yeah. Go out and beat them. That is the best way to get this scenario in order."

Well, lo and behold, probably because the people felt Fatah was corrupt and a whole lot of misdirection on politics and so forth, Hamas beat Fatah.

But to criticize the United States for not pushing an election in the Palestinian Authority when half of the Palestinian territory is controlled by a terrorist organization I think is somewhat duplicitous.

Mr. COTTON. Mr. Wexler, we didn't have the opportunity to overlap. I know your record on these issues. That was long and distinguished.

Can we talk briefly about more fundamental matters? It seems to me, as I have observed for years, first as a civilian, then a soldier, and now a Member of Congress, the fundamental problem is Palestinian rejectionism.

Why is it that Mr. Abbas and Palestinian leadership can't recognize Israel as a Jewish state, in your opinion? Why can't they give up the right to return?

You know, you have a much longer professional experience with these matters and have dealt directly with many of the people involved. I would appreciate your perspective.

Mr. WEXLER. What we have here is nothing less than two competing historical narratives—two peoples, two competing historical narratives. And, unfortunately, the manner in which the Palestinian side thus far—the Arab side, to a large degree, for many decades, essentially viewed this as a zero-sum game. "If we recognize the Jewish national peoples' historical narrative, then our side somehow gets slighted."

And until that is overcome, Prime Minister Netanyahu was right. We are not going to have full peace. That is why it is so important, I believe, for the Palestinians to recognize Israel in the context of being a Jewish state. But we also need to be fair.

If you are going to do that, you have got to tell them where the borders are. Where is the border? Where are the lines of that state?

And we also need to be fair to Prime Minister Netanyahu. He has not asked for recognition of a Jewish state as a precondition. He has said that it should be a part of the complexity of a comprehensive agreement.

And, in that context, if you have a resolution on Jerusalem, if you have a resolution on borders, I am actually confident that the Palestinians, in theory, might be closer to accepting that position.

Mr. COTTON. Yeah. I mean, the fight over narratives goes back beyond just where we are today. I mean, it was treated as great news that Mr. Abbas recognized the Holocaust to have existed and you still have temple denialism as well.

A lot of the issues you raise, though, Yasser Arafat had a chance to accept in 2000, did he not, and he declined it to Bill Clinton and Bill Clinton said that he had made Bill Clinton a failure?

Mr. WEXLER. You are right.

Mr. COTTON. I regret that I am. Thank you.

Mr. DeSANTIS. The gentleman's time is expired.

The votes have been called, but we do have time. So I will recognize my colleague from Florida, Ms. Frankel, for 5 minutes.

Ms. FRANKEL. Thank you, Mr. Chair.

And, first, I want to say welcome to my former colleague in the state legislature and distinguished member of this committee, Mr. Wexler, and recognize also that I have an extraordinary constituent in the audience today who is a dear friend, a remarkable patriot who served us during World War II. He is a great American entrepreneur and an unyielding advocate for Israel for Peace.

Danny Abraham, welcome to you.

Two days ago some of our colleagues here—we went to the floor. We celebrated Israel's 66th Independence Day, its birthday, praised the relationship of the United States and Israel.

And we also noted that the day prior Israelis commemorated Memorial Day to pay tribute to the 24,000-plus Israeli men, women, and children who have lost their lives to the war on terror.

And, you know, we have been to Israel. We know it is beautiful. It is modern and people live good lives, but Israel has never really known real long-lasting peace. There has been intermittent wars, periods of terrorism and so forth.

So there have been a lot of questions and answers today. I will leave you with a real softball question because sometimes we just talk to ourselves.

And for myself and, I know, everyone on the panel, we are true believers in the importance of Israel as our ally and best friend in the Middle East. But I am going to give you each an opportunity to answer the question for the American public.

Why is it so important for Israel to reach a peace agreement with the Palestinians? Why is it important for our country, for the world and, of course, it goes without saying, for Israel?

Mr. WEXLER. I will be happy to start.

Quickly, if you are a Zionist and you believe in the Zionist dream, then Israel needs to figure out a way to separate from the 4- to 5 million Palestinians that live on the West Bank and Gaza.

If Israel is to remain a Jewish and democratic state—a secure Jewish and democratic state, it has got to figure out a way to separate from the Palestinian people.

And the only way to separate, ultimately, that ensures Israel's security is a viable Palestinian state, demilitarized Palestinian state, that is independent and can go on its own.

And in terms of the Palestinians, which is not the purpose of your question, though, for those of us who are Zionists, we must be very careful to recognize also that the Palestinian people have their legitimate rights and also have a historical narrative. And to not do so, I believe, in many ways, morally and ethically, is not consistent with Zionism.

Mr. PRINCE. I would agree with Congressman Wexler's eloquent presentation of why we need to solve this problem, but we do have to take into account that negotiations don't occur in a vacuum.

The equation has to include the Palestinian people, not only their national aspirations, not only the aspirations of the Palestinians in the diaspora and around the world, but also in the West Bank and Gaza.

If you walk into a coffee shop anywhere in the West Bank or in Gaza, Palestinians will talk about national aspirations, but then they will spend 30 minutes talking about how their day-to-day life and the troubles, feeding their family, getting a job, getting the sewage out of their house, getting medical treatments, getting antibiotics, getting adequate care, sending their kids abroad for college.

If there is one thing that the Arab Spring has taught us is that we cannot support dictators in the absence of popular support.

And the Palestinian people did not support this negotiation, not that there wasn't a constituency for peace, but they wanted to clean up their house first and show that there is benefits of peace to the community at large before reaching a final status agreement.

Mr. SCHANZER. I will keep my response short.

I think, look it, Israel promotes American principles and interests in the Middle East. It must have the peace and security that it needs in order to do so. That is in our interest as well as theirs.

Ms. FRANKEL. Thank you very much.

And I yield back my time.

Mr. DESANTIS. I thank the gentlewoman.

And I thank the witnesses. I really appreciate your time, and your comments and testimony are very well received by the members. So thank you so much.

And this hearing stands adjourned.

[Whereupon, at 3:29 p.m., the subcommittee was adjourned.]

APPENDIX

SUBCOMMITTEE HEARING NOTICE
COMMITTEE ON FOREIGN AFFAIRS
U.S. HOUSE OF REPRESENTATIVES
WASHINGTON, DC 20515-6128

Subcommittee on the Middle East and North Africa
Ileana Ros-Lehtinen (R-FL), Chairman

May 1, 2014

TO: MEMBERS OF THE COMMITTEE ON FOREIGN AFFAIRS

You are respectfully requested to attend an OPEN hearing of the Committee on Foreign Affairs to be held by the Subcommittee on the Middle East and North Africa, in Room 2172 of the Rayburn House Office Building (and available live on the Committee website at www.foreignaffairs.house.gov):

DATE: Thursday, May 8, 2014

TIME: 1:45 p.m.

SUBJECT: The Palestinian Authority, Israel and the Peace Process: What's Next?

WITNESSES: Jonathan Schanzer, Ph.D.
                   Vice President for Research
                   Foundation for Defense of Democracies

                   Mr. James Prince
                   Co-founder and President
                   The Democracy Council

                   The Honorable Robert Wexler
                   President
                   S. Daniel Abraham Center for Middle East Peace
                   (Former Member of Congress)

By Direction of the Chairman

The Committee on Foreign Affairs seeks to make its facilities accessible to persons with disabilities. If you are in need of special accommodations, please call 202/225-5021 at least four business days in advance of the event, whenever practicable. Questions with regard to special accommodations in general (including availability of Committee materials in alternative formats and assistive listening devices) may be directed to the Committee.

COMMITTEE ON FOREIGN AFFAIRS

MINUTES OF SUBCOMMITTEE ON _____ *Middle East and North Africa* _____ HEARING

Day __*Thursdsay*__ Date ____*5/8/14*____ Room ____*2172*____

Starting Time ___*1:45 p.m.*___ Ending Time ___*3:29 p.m.*___

Recesses [*0*] (____to ____) (____to ____) (____to ____) (____to ____) (____to ____) (____to ____)

Presiding Member(s)

Chairman Ros-Lehtinen, Rep. DeSantis

Check all of the following that apply:

Open Session ☑   Electronically Recorded (taped) ☑
Executive (closed) Session ☐   Stenographic Record ☑
Televised ☑

TITLE OF HEARING:

The Palestinian Authority, Israel and the Peace Process: What's Next?

SUBCOMMITTEE MEMBERS PRESENT:

(See attendance sheet)

NON-SUBCOMMITTEE MEMBERS PRESENT: *(Mark with an * if they are not members of full committee.)*

None

HEARING WITNESSES: Same as meeting notice attached? Yes ☑ No ☐
(If "no", please list below and include title, agency, department, or organization.)

STATEMENTS FOR THE RECORD: *(List any statements submitted for the record.)*

SFR - Rep. Connolly

TIME SCHEDULED TO RECONVENE _____
or
TIME ADJOURNED ___*3:29 p.m.*___

Subcommittee Staff Director

Hearing Attendance

Hearing Title: The Palestinian Authority, Israel and the Peace Process: What's Next?

Date: 05/08/14

Noncommittee Members

Member	Present
Ros-Lehtinen, Ileana (FL)	X
Chabot, Steve (OH)	X
Wilson, Joe (SC)	
Kinzinger, Adam (IL)	
Cotton, Tom (AR)	X
Weber, Randy (TX)	
Desantis, Ron (FL)	
Collins, Doug (GA)	
Meadows, Mark (NC)	X
Yoho, Ted (FL)	X
Messer, Luke (IN)	

Member	Present
Deutch, Ted (FL)	X
Connolly, Gerald (VA)	X
Higgins, Brian (NY)	X
Cicilline, David (RI)	X
Grayson, Alan (FL)	
Vargas, Juan (CA)	X
Schneider, Bradley (IL)	X
Kennedy, Joseph (MA)	
Meng, Grace (NY)	X
Frankel, Lois (FL)	

Statement for the Record
Submitted by the Honorable Gerald E. Connolly

Mr. Chairman, thank you for holding today's hearing on the current state of affairs with respect to Middle East peace negotiations. I share the concerns expressed by my colleagues, as well as by supporters of both Israelis and Palestinians, over the recent breakdown in the 9-month-old talks, which were brokered by the United States. Once again, we have taken one step forward and two steps back in the effort to obtain a peaceful resolution to this long-standing conflict. Achieving a true two-state solution is in the best interests of the Israeli and Palestinian people, and it is central in U.S. efforts to restore stability within the region.

While there has been no shortage of finger pointing, it appears the collective actions of both sides contributed to the dissolution of the peace talks. The Palestinian Authority resumed the accession process for 15 multilateral treaties and conventions, which it had agreed to suspend for the sake of the peace negotiations. Then it announced a unity agreement with Hamas, which is designated as a terrorist organization by the U.S. and refuses to recognize Israel's legitimacy, completely undermining any chance for serious negotiations. On the other side of the negotiating table, Israel delayed the fourth release of Palestinian prisoners, the final group of 104 total prisoners who Israel agreed to release in exchange for the Palestinian Authority suspending its international recognition efforts. Israel's continued settlement activities were neither helpful nor in the best interests of the talks. Each step back from the table on one side caused the other to respond in kind until the U.S. was left alone in the effort to reach a lasting peace. Knowing how such actions from both sides would be negatively perceived by the other, I would be curious to hear the panel's assessment of whether the U.S. did all that could be done to manage the process.

Irrespective of which party you feel contributed to the demise of these talks, we are now left with serious policy and security questions. As a number of my colleagues touched on during last week's hearing on the Middle East portions of the State Department's FY15 budget, what is to become of U.S. assistance to the Palestinian Authority in the wake of this unity government agreement? Current U.S. law is pretty clear about suspending aid to any power-sharing Palestinian Authority government of which Hamas is a member. In the coming weeks we'll see if the Palestinian Authority is successful in implementing this unity agreement, something on which it has not been able to deliver after previous unity announcements. In the meantime, what is the State Department doing to encourage or ensure that any unity government involving Hamas meets the Quartet Principles of recognizing Israel, renouncing terrorism, and respecting past agreements? In addition, how will the U.S. respond to further attempts by the unity government to achieve international recognition should it not meet the Quartet Principles? The U.S. already suspended dues and lost its voting rights within the United Nations Educational, Scientific and Cultural Organization (UNESCO) over this very issue. Loss of U.S. input at UNESCO is not trivial. Are we willing to continue with that policy, even if doing so further conflicts with U.S. interests abroad?

We also need to be mindful of the situation on the ground in the wake of this agreement. President Obama has characterized the ongoing conflict between Israel and the Palestinian Authority as "combustible." Short of a change in philosophy within Hamas, Israeli leaders will be under even more pressure to take a strong stance against the new Palestinian Authority unity government. What will that mean for Palestinians living in the West Bank, for example? There are also questions about whether this unity government will be able to function. In addition to the potential loss of U.S. and other international assistance, there is the considerable challenge of bridging the differences and basic public needs between the Fatah-led West Bank and the Hamas-led Gaza Strip. And we cannot overlook the motivations of Hamas in this situation. Hamas' influence has been waning in places like Egypt, Turkey, and other countries in the region. The U.S. needs to guard against Hamas using this unity government effort as a foothold for its radical agenda and further drive a wedge into any semblance that remains of this peace process.

I welcome the panel's insights into what other factors may have contributed to the breakdown in these recent negotiations, but, more important, I would like your input on what issues this Committee and the Congress should consider in taking further actions to guide the U.S. response moving forward.